Mastering Xamarin.F
Second Edition

Build rich, maintainable, multi-platform, native mobile apps
with Xamarin.Forms

Ed Snider

BIRMINGHAM - MUMBAI

Mastering Xamarin.Forms
Second Edition

Commissioning Editor: Smeet Thakkar
Acquisition Editor: Tushar Gupta
Content Development Editor: Jason Pereira
Technical Editor: Rutuja Vaze
Copy Editor: Dhanya Baburaj
Project Coordinator: Sheejal Shah
Proofreader: Safis Editing
Indexer: Rekha Nair
Graphics: Jason Monteiro
Production Coordinator: Shantanu Zagade

First published: January 2016
Second edition: March 2018

Production reference: 1210318

Published by Packt Publishing Ltd.
Livery Place
35 Livery Street
Birmingham
B3 2PB, UK.

ISBN 978-1-78829-026-5

www.packtpub.com

In memory of my friend and colleague, Ed Buhain.

`mapt.io`

Mapt is an online digital library that gives you full access to over 5,000 books and videos, as well as industry leading tools to help you plan your personal development and advance your career. For more information, please visit our website.

Why subscribe?

- Spend less time learning and more time coding with practical eBooks and Videos from over 4,000 industry professionals

- Improve your learning with Skill Plans built especially for you

- Get a free eBook or video every month

- Mapt is fully searchable

- Copy and paste, print, and bookmark content

PacktPub.com

Did you know that Packt offers eBook versions of every book published, with PDF and ePub files available? You can upgrade to the eBook version at `www.PacktPub.com` and as a print book customer, you are entitled to a discount on the eBook copy. Get in touch with us at `service@packtpub.com` for more details.

At `www.PacktPub.com`, you can also read a collection of free technical articles, sign up for a range of free newsletters, and receive exclusive discounts and offers on Packt books and eBooks.

Foreword

I'll never forget coming down the escalator of the Xamarin Evolve 2014 venue in Atlanta. Two fantastical things happened. My brand new iPhone in a slim case slipped my grip and went tumbling end over end down the metal escalator steps. By the second bounce I'd given up any hope that it wasn't completely destroyed. As it reached the bottom I could see it bumping up against the end as the steps disappeared. To my complete amazement the gorilla glass was unblemished and the only sign of damage was a little nick in the bezel. As I celebrated wildly and repeatedly shouted "did you see that?!", I noticed a developer engaged in passionate conversation with a Xamarin employee. They were totally oblivious to my miracle. What could be so much more captivating? Then I heard it. "This Xamarin.Forms thing is amazing. So, could I build a game with it?! I have this game...." I shook my head. Who would think to do THAT with Xamarin.Forms? Who would think it would be a good idea?!

I heard variations of that same conversation many times over the following days, and in the years since. This is the lesson I continue to learn: when developers are inspired by what you do, they will dream bigger than you imagine. Xamarin continues to fuel dreams, and your dreams in turn propel Xamarin into the future. Today, as a now open source product, you are contributing amazing things to Xamarin.Forms, bringing it to WPF, Linux, IoT, and even the web. The web!

With so many opportunities and possibilities provided by Xamarin, it's easy to get lost searching for the "right" or "best practices" or just plain effective way to do anything. For this reason I'm ever grateful for books like this from Ed where he takes his practical experience building applications and helps us navigate this ever growing landscape of cross-platform development.

I'm in an enviable position now as a Senior Program Manager at Microsoft for Xamarin.Forms to witness many of the amazing applications being developed using Xamarin.Forms, and I'm truly inspired by what you're doing. Keep up the great work!

David Ortinau
Senior Program Manager, Xamarin.Forms
Microsoft

Contributors

About the author

Ed Snider is a senior software developer, speaker, author, and Microsoft MVP based in the Washington D.C./Northern Virginia area. He has a passion for mobile design and development and regularly speaks about Xamarin and Windows app development in the community. Ed works at InfernoRed Technology, where his primary role is working with clients and partners to build mobile and media focused products on iOS, Android, and Windows. He started working with the .NET framework in 2005 when .NET 2.0 came out and has been building mobile apps with .NET since 2011. Ed blogs at `edsnider.net` and can be found on Twitter at `twitter.com/edsnider`.

Acknowledgments

I would like to acknowledge the many people without whom this book would not have been possible:

My parents, my wife Kelly, and my daughters Camden and Colby for their loving support and encouragement.

Scott, Art, Josh, and all my teammates at InfernoRed Technology for always inspiring and supporting me.

Joseph Hill, David Ortinau, Jayme Singleton, James Montemagno, and everyone at Xamarin for all of their support through the years.

My friend and fellow MVP, Dan Hermes, for his support, guidance, and encouragement.

My friend and colleague, Roberto Hernandez, for his invaluable technical review of this book.

About the reviewer

Roberto Hernandez is a developer, speaker and all-round tech enthusiast with 18 years of experience in the software industry. Roberto resides in Northern Virginia, where he participates as a speaker at user groups and conferences all through the Mid-Atlantic. Recognized as a Microsoft MVP for C# in 2007, 2008, 2010, he is a member of the Microsoft MVP reConnect. Roberto works as a Developer Extraordinaire at InfernoRed Technology focused on building Mobile and Cloud solutions. You can follow his latest interest at his blog at OverrideThis or follow him on Twitter at @hernandezrobert.

> *To my Mother, who at the time did not know what a computer looked like but decided anyway to enroll an 8 year old boy, and his two sisters, in after-school computer programming lessons, which led to a lifelong passionate interest in technology and learning. To my wife, who supports my obnoxious obsession with technology, and to my beautiful daughters who make my life special every day.*

Packt is searching for authors like you

If you're interested in becoming an author for Packt, please visit authors.packtpub.com and apply today. We have worked with thousands of developers and tech professionals, just like you, to help them share their insight with the global tech community. You can make a general application, apply for a specific hot topic that we are recruiting an author for, or submit your own idea.

Table of Contents

Preface

Xamarin released the Xamarin.Forms toolkit in the summer of 2014, and it has since become a very popular framework for .NET mobile app developers. On the surface, Xamarin.Forms is a user interface toolkit focused on abstracting the platform-specific UI APIs of iOS, Android, and Windows into a single easy-to-use set of APIs. In addition, Xamarin.Forms also provides the common components of a Model-View-ViewModel (MVVM) framework, making it extremely easy and intuitive to bind data to a user interface.

Xamarin.Forms comes with several building blocks that are paramount to a solid mobile app architecture, such as dependency injection, data binding, messaging, and navigation. However, many apps will quickly outgrow these *in the box* capabilities and require the use of more advanced and sophisticated replacements. This book will show you how to leverage the strengths of the Xamarin.Forms toolkit while complementing it with popular patterns and libraries to achieve a more robust and sustainable app architecture.

As with any framework or toolkit, there are specific scenarios where Xamarin.Forms might make more sense than others. Xamarin has done a great job of providing guidance and recommendations on when the use of Xamarin.Forms is appropriate versus when it might be a better decision to use the core Xamarin platform. Once you have made the decision to use Xamarin.Forms, this book will help guide you through using patterns and best practices with your Xamarin.Forms mobile app by walking you through an end-to-end example.

Who this book is for

This book is intended for .NET developers who are familiar with the Xamarin platform and Xamarin.Forms toolkit. If you have already started working with Xamarin.Forms and want to take your app to the next level, making it more maintainable, testable, and flexible, then this book is for you.

What this book covers

`Chapter 1`, *Getting Started*, will start off by quickly reviewing the basics of the Xamarin.Forms toolkit. We will then walk through building a simple app with Xamarin.Forms, called TripLog. The TripLog app will serve as the foundation that we build upon throughout the rest of the book by applying new techniques and concepts in each subsequent chapter.

Chapter 2, *MVVM and Data Binding*, will introduce the Model-View-ViewModel (MVVM) pattern and the benefits of using it in a mobile app architecture. We will then walk through updating the TripLog app with ViewModels that provide data context for the app's pages through data binding.

Chapter 3, *Navigation*, will explain how navigation works in Xamarin.Forms and some approaches to navigation related to MVVM. We will build a custom navigation service for the TripLog app that extends the one provided by Xamarin.Forms to provide a navigation model that occurs solely at the ViewModel level, decoupled from the pages themselves.

Chapter 4, *Platform Specific Services and Dependency Injection*, will discuss the power of the inversion of control (IoC) and the dependency injection pattern, specific to multi-platform mobile app development. We will discuss the Xamarin.Forms Dependency Service and some of its shortcomings. We will add a third-party dependency injection library to the TripLog app, in the place of Xamarin.Forms's default Dependency Service. We will then build some services that are dependent on platform-specific APIs and use them within the TripLog app through dependency injection.

Chapter 5, *User Interface*, will explain how to tap into platform-specific APIs using custom renderers in Xamarin.Forms. We will also discuss the use of value converters to customize the appearance of data at the time of binding.

Chapter 6, *API Data Access*, will explain how to set up a new RESTful API using a Microsoft Azure App Service. We will then walk through how to connect the TripLog app to the API to get its data and how to set up caching for offline use.

Chapter 7, *Authentication*, will explain how to set up authentication on the API created in Chapter 6, *API Data Access*, and then how to add sign in and authentication to the TripLog app.

Chapter 8, *Testing*, will discuss the importance of testing in mobile apps. We will walk through how to take advantage of the patterns introduced throughout the book to easily unit test the ViewModels within the TripLog app.

Chapter 9, *App Monitoring*, will explain the importance of crash reporting and collecting analytical data in mobile apps. We will then integrate the Visual Studio App Center SDK into the TripLog app using the service dependency pattern implemented in Chapter 4, *Platform Specific Services and Dependency Injection*.

Because the focus of this book is on applying patterns and best practices to apps built with Xamarin.Forms and not on the actual specifics of Xamarin.Forms, the chapters will only use a single platform, iOS, for simplicity. However, the architectural concepts in the book will apply to all platforms, and any platform-specific code, such as platform services or custom renderers, will be included for iOS, Android, and UWP with the example code that is available for download with the purchase of this book.

To get the most out of this book

To get the most out of this book, you should have a working knowledge of the Xamarin platform and Xamarin.Forms toolkit as well as experience with .NET.

In order to follow along with the code throughout this book, you will need to have Visual Studio and Xamarin installed on your Windows or Mac machine. Although the examples throughout this book are shown in Visual Studio for Mac, everything shown can also be done in Visual Studio for Windows. If you are using a Windows machine, you will need a Mac running Xamarin on your network to serve as a build host to build and deploy iOS apps. For details on setting up a Mac build host or any other requirements for setting up a Xamarin development environment, visit `docs.microsoft.com/en-us/xamarin`.

In `Chapter 6`, *API Data Access*, you will need a Microsoft Azure account in order to follow along with the examples to create a basic API using an Azure App Service.

Throughout this book, there are several tools and libraries used, which are obtained from NuGet via the Visual Studio package manager.

Download the example code files

You can download the example code files for this book from your account at `www.packtpub.com`. If you purchased this book elsewhere, you can visit `www.packtpub.com/support` and register to have the files emailed directly to you.

You can download the code files by following these steps:

1. Log in or register at `www.packtpub.com`.
2. Select the **SUPPORT** tab.
3. Click on **Code Downloads & Errata**.
4. Enter the name of the book in the **Search** box and follow the onscreen instructions.

Once the file is downloaded, please make sure that you unzip or extract the folder using the latest version of:

- WinRAR/7-Zip for Windows
- Zipeg/iZip/UnRarX for Mac
- 7-Zip/PeaZip for Linux

The code bundle for the book is also hosted on GitHub at `www.github.com/PacktPublishing/Mastering-Xamarin.Forms-Second-Edition`. We also have other code bundles from our rich catalog of books and videos available at `www.github.com/PacktPublishing`. Check them out!

Conventions used

There are a number of text conventions used throughout this book.

`CodeInText`: Indicates code words in text, class names, property names, field names, folder names, filenames, file extensions, pathnames, URLs, and user input. Here is an example: "Create a new folder in the core project named `Models`."

A block of code is set as follows:

```
public abstract class BaseViewModel
{
    protected BaseViewModel ()
    { }
}
```

When we wish to draw your attention to a particular part of a code block, the relevant lines or items are set in bold:

```
public App()
{
    InitializeComponent();
    MainPage = new NavigationPage(new TripLog.MainPage());
}
```

Bold: Indicates a new term, an important word, or words that you see onscreen. For example, words in menus or dialog boxes appear in the text like this. Here is an example: "In Visual Studio, click on **File | New Solution**."

 Warnings or important notes appear like this.

 Tips and tricks appear like this.

Get in touch

Feedback from our readers is always welcome.

General feedback: Email `feedback@packtpub.com` and mention the book title in the subject of your message. If you have questions about any aspect of this book, please email us at `questions@packtpub.com`.

Errata: Although we have taken every care to ensure the accuracy of our content, mistakes do happen. If you have found a mistake in this book, we would be grateful if you would report this to us. Please visit `www.packtpub.com/submit-errata`, selecting your book, clicking on the Errata Submission Form link, and entering the details.

Piracy: If you come across any illegal copies of our works in any form on the Internet, we would be grateful if you would provide us with the location address or website name. Please contact us at `copyright@packtpub.com` with a link to the material.

If you are interested in becoming an author: If there is a topic that you have expertise in and you are interested in either writing or contributing to a book, please visit `authors.packtpub.com`.

Reviews

Please leave a review. Once you have read and used this book, why not leave a review on the site that you purchased it from? Potential readers can then see and use your unbiased opinion to make purchase decisions, we at Packt can understand what you think about our products, and our authors can see your feedback on their book. Thank you!

For more information about Packt, please visit packtpub.com.

1
Getting Started

The goal of this book is to focus on how to apply best practices and patterns to mobile apps built with **Xamarin.Forms**, and not on the actual Xamarin.Forms toolkit and API itself. The best way to achieve this goal is to build an app end to end, applying new concepts in each chapter. Therefore, the goal of this chapter is to simply put together the basic structure of a Xamarin.Forms mobile app codebase, which will serve as a foundation that we can build from throughout the rest of this book.

In this chapter, we will do the following:

- Introduce and define the features of the app that we will build throughout the rest of the book
- Create a new Xamarin.Forms mobile app with an initial app structure and user interface

Introducing the app idea

Just like the beginning of many new mobile projects, we will start with an idea.
We will create a travel app named **TripLog** and, like the name suggests, it will be an app
that will allow its users to log their travel adventures. Although the app itself will not solve
any real-world problems, it will have features that will require us to solve real-world
architecture and coding problems. The app will take advantage of several core concepts
such as list views, maps, location services, and live data from a RESTful API, and we will
apply patterns and best practices throughout this book to implement these concepts.

Defining features

Before we get started, it is important to understand the requirements and features of the
TripLog app. We will do this by quickly defining some of the high-level things this app will
allow its users to do:

- View existing log entries (online and offline)
- Add new log entries with the following data:
  - Title
  - Location using GPS
  - Date
  - Notes
  - Rating
- Sign into the app

Creating the initial app

To start off the new TripLog mobile app project, we will need to create the initial solution
architecture. We can also create the core shell of our app's user interface by creating the
initial screens based on the basic features we have just defined.

Setting up the solution

We will start things off by creating a brand new, blank Xamarin.Forms solution within Visual Studio by performing the following steps:

1. In Visual Studio, click on **File | New Solution**. This will bring up a series of dialog screens that will walk you through creating a new Xamarin.Forms solution. On the first dialog, click on **App** on the left-hand side, under the **Multiplatform** section, and then select **Blank Forms App**, as shown in the following screenshot:

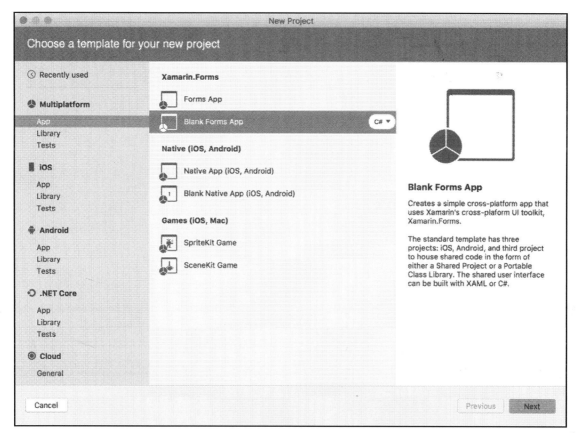

2. On the next dialog screen, enter the name of the app, `TripLog`, ensure that **Use Portable Class Library** is selected for the **Shared Code** option, and that **Use XAML for user interface files** option is checked, as shown in the following screenshot:

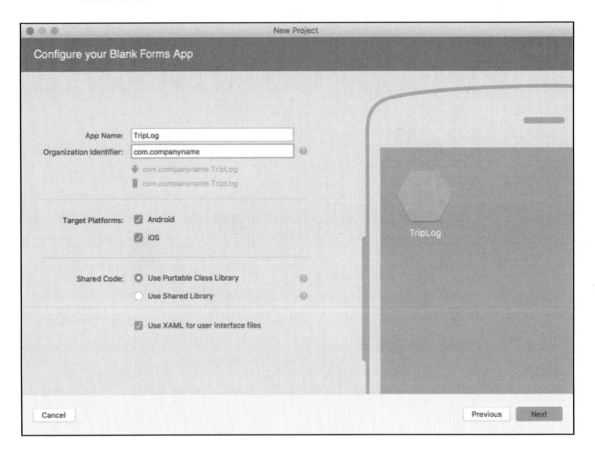

 The Xamarin.Forms project template in Visual Studio for Windows will use a .NET Standard library instead of a Portable Class Library for its core library project. As of the writing of this book, the Visual Studio for Mac templates still use a Portable Class Library.

3. On the final dialog screen, simply click on the **Create** button, as follows:

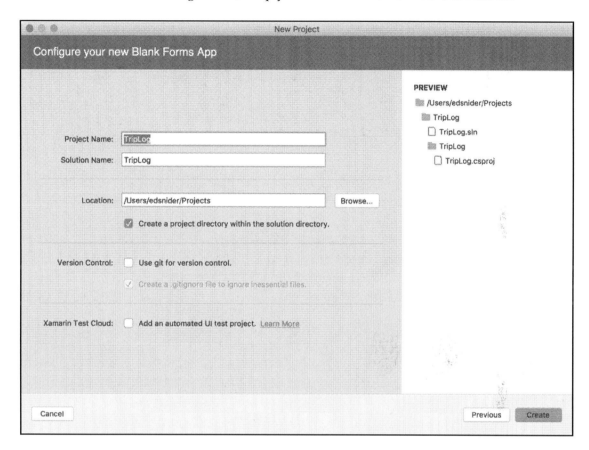

After creating the new Xamarin.Forms solution, you will have several projects created within it, as shown in the following screenshot:

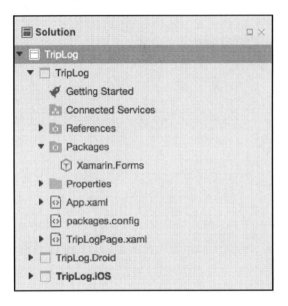

There will be a single portable class library project and two platform-specific projects, as follows:

- **TripLog**: This is a portable class library project that will serve as the *core* layer of the solution architecture. This is the layer that will include all our business logic, data objects, Xamarin.Forms pages, and other non-platform-specific code. The code in this project is common and not specific to a platform, and can therefore, be shared across the platform projects.
- **TripLog.iOS**: This is the iOS platform-specific project containing all the code and assets required to build and deploy the iOS app from this solution. By default, it will have a reference to the TripLog core project.
- **TripLog.Droid**: This is the Android platform-specific project containing all the code and assets required to build and deploy the Android app from this solution. By default, it will have a reference to the TripLog core project.

If you are using Visual Studio for Mac, you will only get an iOS and an Android project when you create a new Xamarin.Forms solution. To include a Windows (UWP) app in your Xamarin.Forms solution, you will need to use Visual Studio for Windows. Although the screenshots and samples used throughout this book are demonstrated using Visual Studio for Mac, the code and concepts will also work in Visual Studio for Windows. Refer to the Preface of this book for further details on software and hardware requirements that need to be met to follow along with the concepts in this book.

You'll notice a file in the core library named App.xaml, which includes a code-behind class in App.xaml.cs named App that inherits from Xamarin.Forms.Application. Initially, the App constructor sets the MainPage property to a new instance of a ContentPage named TripLogPage that simply displays some default text.

The first thing we will do in our TripLog app is build the initial views, or screens, required for our UI, and then update that MainPage property of the App class in App.xaml.cs.

Updating the Xamarin.Forms packages

If you expand the Packages folder within each of the projects in the solution, you will see that Xamarin.Forms is a NuGet package that is automatically included when we select the Xamarin.Forms project template. It is possible that the included NuGet packages need to be updated. Ensure that you update them in each of the projects within the solution so that you are using the latest version of Xamarin.Forms.

Creating the main page

The main page of the app will serve as the entry point into the app and will display a list of existing trip log entries. Our trip log entries will be represented by a data model named TripLogEntry. Models are a key pillar in the Model-View-ViewModel (MVVM) pattern and data binding, which we will explore more in Chapter 2, *MVVM and Data Binding*; however, in this chapter, we will create a simple class that will represent the TripLogEntry model.

Let us now start creating the main page by performing the following steps:

1. First, add a new Xamarin.Forms XAML ContentPage to the core project and name it MainPage.

2. Next, update the `MainPage` property of the `App` class in `App.xaml.cs` to a new instance of `Xamarin.Forms.NavigationPage` whose root is a new instance of `TripLog.MainPage` that we just created:

```
public App()
{
    InitializeComponent();
    MainPage = new NavigationPage(new MainPage());
}
```

3. Delete `TripLogPage.xaml` from the core project as it is no longer needed.
4. Create a new folder in the core project named `Models`.
5. Create a new empty class file in the `Models` folder named `TripLogEntry`.
6. Update the `TripLogEntry` class with auto-implemented properties representing the attributes of an entry:

```
public class TripLogEntry
{
    public string Title { get; set; }
    public double Latitude { get; set; }
    public double Longitude { get; set; }
    public DateTime Date { get; set; }
    public int Rating { get; set; }
    public string Notes { get; set; }
}
```

7. Now that we have a model to represent our trip log entries, we can use it to display some trips on the main page using a `ListView` control. We will use a `DataTemplate` to describe how the model data should be displayed in each of the rows in the `ListView` using the following XAML in the `ContentPage.Content` tag in `MainPage.xaml`:

```
<ContentPage xmlns="http://xamarin.com/schemas/2014/forms"
    xmlns:x="http://schemas.microsoft.com/winfx/2009/xaml"
    x:Class="TripLog.MainPage"
    Title="TripLog">
    <ContentPage.Content>
        <ListView x:Name="trips">
            <ListView.ItemTemplate>
                <DataTemplate>
                    <TextCell Text="{Binding Title}"
                              Detail="{Binding Notes}" />
                </DataTemplate>
            </ListView.ItemTemplate>
        </ListView>
```

```
     </ListView>
   </ContentPage.Content>
</ContentPage>
```

8. In the main page's code-behind, `MainPage.xaml.cs`, we will populate the `ListView ItemsSource` with a hard-coded collection of `TripLogEntry` objects. In the next chapter, we will move this collection to the page's data context (that is its ViewModel), and in Chapter 6, *API Data Access*, we will replace this hard-coded data with data from a live Azure backend:

```
public partial class MainPage : ContentPage
{
    public MainPage()
    {
        InitializeComponent();

        var items = new List<TripLogEntry>
        {
            new TripLogEntry
            {
                Title = "Washington Monument",
                Notes = "Amazing!",
                Rating = 3,
                Date = new DateTime(2017, 2, 5),
                Latitude = 38.8895,
                Longitude = -77.0352
            },
            new TripLogEntry
            {
                Title = "Statue of Liberty",
                Notes = "Inspiring!",
                Rating = 4,
                Date = new DateTime(2017, 4, 13),
                Latitude = 40.6892,
                Longitude = -74.0444
            },
            new TripLogEntry
            {
                Title = "Golden Gate Bridge",
                Notes = "Foggy, but beautiful.",
                Rating = 5,
                Date = new DateTime(2017, 4, 26),
                Latitude = 37.8268,
                Longitude = -122.4798
            }
        };
```

```
        trips.ItemsSource = items;
    }
}
```

At this point, we have a single page that is displayed as the app's main page. If we debug the app and run it in a simulator, emulator, or on a physical device, we should see the main page showing the list of log entries we hard-coded into the view, as shown in the following screenshot.

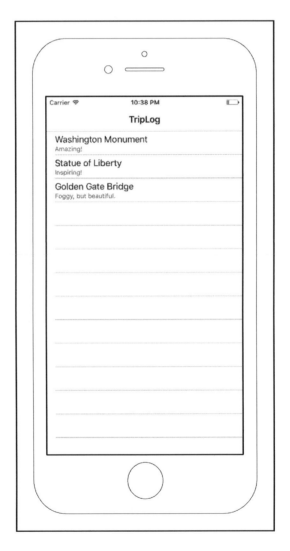

In Chapter 2, *MVVM and Data Binding*, we will refactor this quite a bit as we implement MVVM and leverage the benefits of data binding.

Creating the new entry page

The new entry page of the app will give the user a way to add a new log entry by presenting a series of fields to collect the log entry details. There are several ways to build a form to collect data in Xamarin.Forms. You can simply use a StackLayout and present a stack of Label and Entry controls on the screen, or you can also use a TableView with various types of ViewCell elements. In most cases, a TableView will give you a very nice default, platform-specific look and feel. However, if your design calls for a more customized aesthetic, you might be better off leveraging the other layout options available in Xamarin.Forms. For the purpose of this app, we will use a TableView.

There are some key data points we need to collect when our users log new entries with the app, such as title, location, date, rating, and notes. For now, we will use a regular EntryCell element for each of these fields. We will update, customize, and add things to these fields later in this book. For example, we will wire the location fields to a geolocation service that will automatically determine the location. We will also update the date field to use an actual platform-specific date picker control. For now, we will just focus on building the basic app shell.

In order to create the new entry page that contains a TableView, perform the following steps:

1. First, add a new Xamarin.Forms XAML ContentPage to the core project and name it NewEntryPage.

2. Update the new entry page using the following XAML to build the TableView that will represent the data entry form on the page:

```
<ContentPage xmlns="http://xamarin.com/schemas/2014/forms"
    xmlns:x="http://schemas.microsoft.com/winfx/2009/xaml"
    x:Class="TripLog.NewEntryPage"
    Title="New Entry">
    <ContentPage.Content>
        <TableView Intent="Form">
            <TableView.Root>
                <TableSection>
                    <EntryCell Label="Title" />
                    <EntryCell Label="Latitude"
                                Keyboard="Numeric" />
                    <EntryCell Label="Longitude"
```

```
                              Keyboard="Numeric" />
            <EntryCell Label="Date" />
            <EntryCell Label="Rating"
                              Keyboard="Numeric" />
            <EntryCell Label="Notes" />
          </TableSection>
        </TableView.Root>
      </TableView>
    </ContentPage.Content>
  </ContentPage>
```

Now that we have created the new entry page, we need to add a way for users to get to this new screen from the main page. We will do this by adding a **New** button to the main page's toolbar. In Xamarin.Forms, this is accomplished by adding a `ToolbarItem` to the `ContentPage.ToolbarItems` collection and wiring up the `ToolbarItem.Clicked` event to navigate to the new entry page, as shown in the following XAML:

```
<!-- MainPage.xaml -->
<ContentPage>
    <ContentPage.ToolbarItems>
        <ToolbarItem Text="New" Clicked="New_Clicked" />
    </ContentPage.ToolbarItems>
</ContentPage>

// MainPage.xaml.cs
public partial class MainPage : ContentPage
{
    // ...

    void New_Clicked(object sender, EventArgs e)
    {
        Navigation.PushAsync(new NewEntryPage());
    }
}
```

In Chapter 3, *Navigation*, we will build a custom service to handle navigation between pages and will replace the `Clicked` event with a data-bound `ICommand ViewModel` property, but for now, we will use the default Xamarin.Forms navigation mechanism.

When we run the app, we will see a **New** button on the toolbar of the main page. Clicking on the **New** button should bring us to the new entry page, as shown in the following screenshot:

We will need to add a save button to the new entry page toolbar so that we can save new items. For now, this button will just be a placeholder in the UI that we will bind an ICommand to in Chapter 2, *MVVM and Data Binding*. The save button will be added to the new entry page toolbar in the same way the **New** button was added to the main page toolbar. Update the XAML in NewEntryPage.xaml to include a new ToolbarItem, as shown in the following code:

```
<ContentPage>
    <ContentPage.ToolbarItems>
        <ToolbarItem Text="Save" />
    </ContentPage.ToolbarItems>
    <!-- ... -->
</ContentPage>
```

When we run the app again and navigate to the new entry page, we should now see the **Save** button on the toolbar, as shown in the following screenshot:

Creating the entry detail page

When a user clicks on one of the log entry items on the main page, we want to take them to a page that displays more details about that particular item, including a map that plots the item's location. Along with additional details and a more in-depth view of the item, a detail page is also a common area where actions on that item might take place, such as, editing the item or sharing the item on social media. The detail page will take an instance of a TripLogEntry model as a constructor parameter, which we will use in the rest of the page to display the entry details to the user.

In order to create the entry detail page, perform the following steps:

1. First, add a new Xamarin.Forms XAML ContentPage to the project and name it DetailPage.

2. Update the constructor of the DetailPage class in DetailPage.xaml.cs to take a TripLogEntry parameter named entry, as shown in the following code:

```
public class DetailPage : ContentPage
{
    public DetailPage(TripLogEntry entry)
    {
        // ...
    }
}
```

3. Add the **Xamarin.Forms.Maps** NuGet package to the core project and to each of the platform-specific projects. This separate NuGet package is required in order to use the Xamarin.Forms Map control in the next step.

4. Update the XAML in DetailPage.xaml to include a Grid layout to display a Map control and some Label controls to display the trip's details, as shown in the following code:

```
<ContentPage xmlns="http://xamarin.com/schemas/2014/forms"
    xmlns:x="http://schemas.microsoft.com/winfx/2009/xaml"
    xmlns:maps="clr-
namespace:Xamarin.Forms.Maps;assembly=Xamarin.Forms.Maps"
    x:Class="TripLog.DetailPage">
    <ContentPage.Content>
        <Grid>
            <Grid.RowDefinitions>
                <RowDefinition Height="4*" />
                <RowDefinition Height="Auto" />
                <RowDefinition Height="1*" />
            </Grid.RowDefinitions>
```

```
<maps:Map x:Name="map" Grid.RowSpan="3" />

<BoxView Grid.Row="1" BackgroundColor="White"
         Opacity=".8" />

<StackLayout Padding="10" Grid.Row="1">
    <Label x:Name="title" HorizontalOptions="Center" />
    <Label x:Name="date" HorizontalOptions="Center" />
    <Label x:Name="rating" HorizontalOptions="Center" />
    <Label x:Name="notes" HorizontalOptions="Center" />
</StackLayout>
    </Grid>
</ContentPage.Content>
</ContentPage>
```

5. Update the detail page's code-behind, `DetailPage.xaml.cs`, to center the map and plot the trip's location. We also need to update the `Label` controls on the detail page with the properties of the `entry` constructor parameter:

```
public DetailPage(TripLogEntry entry)
{
    InitializeComponent();

    map.MoveToRegion(MapSpan.FromCenterAndRadius(
        new Position(entry.Latitude, entry.Longitude),
        Distance.FromMiles(.5)));

    map.Pins.Add(new Pin
    {
        Type = PinType.Place,
        Label = entry.Title,
        Position = new Position(entry.Latitude, entry.Longitude)
    });

    title.Text = entry.Title;
    date.Text = entry.Date.ToString("M");
    rating.Text = $"{entry.Rating} star rating";
    notes.Text = entry.Notes;
}
```

6. Next, we need to wire up the `ItemTapped` event of the `ListView` on the main page to pass the tapped item over to the entry detail page that we have just created, as shown in the following code:

```
<!-- MainPage.xaml -->
<ListView x:Name="trips" ItemTapped="Trips_ItemTapped">
    <!-- ... -->
</ListView>

// MainPage.xaml.cs
public MainPage()
{
    // ...

    async void Trips_ItemTapped(object sender, ItemTappedEventArgs e)
    {
        var trip = (TripLogEntry)e.Item;
        await Navigation.PushAsync(new DetailPage(trip));

        // Clear selection
        trips.SelectedItem = null;
    }
}
```

7. Finally, we will need to initialize the Xamarin.Forms.Maps library in each platform-specific startup class (`AppDelegate` for iOS and `MainActivity` for Android) using the following code:

```
// in iOS AppDelegate
global::Xamarin.Forms.Forms.Init();
Xamarin.FormsMaps.Init();
LoadApplication(new App());

// in Android MainActivity
global::Xamarin.Forms.Forms.Init(this, bundle);
Xamarin.FormsMaps.Init(this, bundle);
LoadApplication(new App());
```

Now, when we run the app and tap on one of the log entries on the main page, it will navigate us to the details page to see more detail about that particular log entry, as shown in the following screenshot:

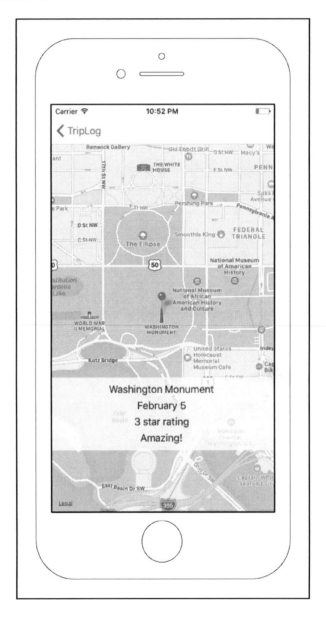

Summary

In this chapter, we built a simple three-page app with static data, leveraging the most basic concepts of the Xamarin.Forms toolkit. We used the default Xamarin.Forms navigation APIs to move between the three pages, which we will refactor in `Chapter 3`, *Navigation*, to use a more flexible, custom navigation approach.

Now that we have built the foundation of the app, including the basic UI for each page within the app, we'll begin enhancing the app with better architecture design patterns, live data with offline syncing, nicer looking UI elements, and tests. In the next chapter, we will introduce the MVVM pattern and data binding to the app to enforce a separation between the user interface layer and the business and data access logic.

2
MVVM and Data Binding

In this chapter, we will take a look at the **Model-View-ViewModel** (**MVVM**) pattern, the MVVM elements that are offered with the Xamarin.Forms toolkit, and how we can expand on them to truly take advantage of the power of the pattern. As we dig into these topics, we will apply what we have learned to the TripLog app that we started building in Chapter 1, *Getting Started*.

In this chapter, we will cover the following topics:

- Understanding the MVVM pattern and data binding
- MVVM in the Xamarin.Forms toolkit
- Adding the MVVM pattern and data binding to the Xamarin.Forms mobile app created in Chapter 1, *Getting Started*

Understanding the MVVM pattern

At its core, MVVM is a presentation pattern designed to control the separation between user interfaces and the rest of an application. The key elements of the MVVM pattern are as follows:

- **Models**: Models represent the business entities of an application. When responses come back from an API, they are typically deserialized to models.
- **Views**: Views represent the actual pages or screens of an application, along with all of the elements that make them up, including custom controls. Views are very platform-specific and depend heavily on platform APIs to render the application's **user interface** (**UI**).

- **ViewModels**: ViewModels control and manipulate the Views by serving as their data context. ViewModels are made up of a series of properties represented by Models. These properties are part of what is bound to the Views to provide the data that is displayed to users, or to collect the data that is entered or selected by users. In addition to model-backed properties, ViewModels can also contain commands, which are action-backed properties that bind the actual functionality and execution to events that occur in the Views, such as button taps or list item selections.

- **Data binding**: Data binding is the concept of connecting data properties and actions in a ViewModel with the user interface elements in a View. The actual implementation of how data binding happens can vary and, in most cases is provided by a framework, toolkit, or library. In Windows app development, data binding is provided declaratively in XAML. In traditional (non-Xamarin.Forms) Xamarin app development, data binding is either a manual process or dependent on a framework such as **MvvmCross** (`https://github.com/MvvmCross/ MvvmCross`), a popular framework in the .NET mobile development community. Data binding in Xamarin.Forms follows a very similar approach to Windows app development.

Adding MVVM to the app

The first step of introducing MVVM into an app is to set up the structure by adding folders that will represent the core tenants of the pattern, such as Models, ViewModels, and Views. Traditionally, the Models and ViewModels live in a core library (usually, a portable class library or .NET standard library), whereas the Views live in a platform-specific library. Thanks to the power of the Xamarin.Forms toolkit and its abstraction of platform-specific UI APIs, the Views in a Xamarin.Forms app can also live in the core library.

Just because the Views can live in the core library with the ViewModels and Models, this doesn't mean that separation between the user interface and the app logic isn't important.

When implementing a specific structure to support a design pattern, it is helpful to have your application namespaces organized in a similar structure. This is not a requirement but it is something that can be useful. By default, Visual Studio for Mac will associate namespaces with directory names, as shown in the following screenshot:

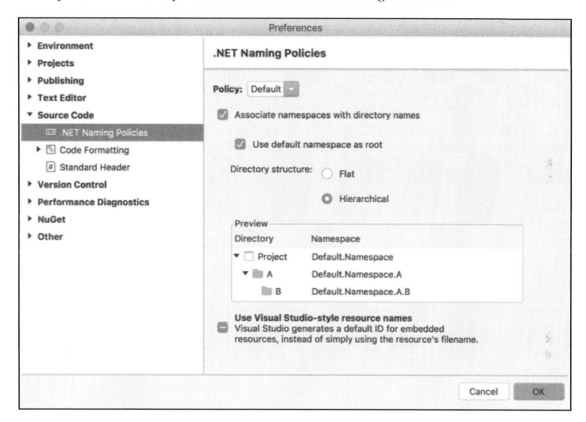

Setting up the app structure

For the TripLog app, we will let the Views, ViewModels, and Models all live in the same core portable class library. In our solution, this is the project called TripLog. We have already added a `Models` folder in Chapter 1, *Getting Started*, so we just need to add a `ViewModels` folder and a `Views` folder to the project to complete the MVVM structure. In order to set up the app structure, perform the following steps:

1. Add a new folder named `ViewModels` to the root of the TripLog project.
2. Add a new folder named `Views` to the root of the TripLog project.

3. Move the existing XAML pages files (`MainPage.xaml`, `DetailPage.xaml`, and `NewEntryPage.xaml` and their `.cs` code-behind files) into the `Views` folder that we have just created.

4. Update the namespace of each Page from `TripLog` to `TripLog.Views`.

5. Update the `x:Class` attribute of each Page's root `ContentPage` from `TripLog.MainPage`, `TripLog.DetailPage`, and `TripLog.NewEntryPage` to `TripLog.Views.MainPage`, `TripLog.Views.DetailPage`, and `TripLog.Views.NewEntryPage`, respectively.

6. Update the `using` statements on any class that references the Pages. Currently, this should only be in the `App` class in `App.xaml.cs`, where `MainPage` is instantiated.

Once the MVVM structure has been added, the folder structure in the solution should look similar to the following screenshot:

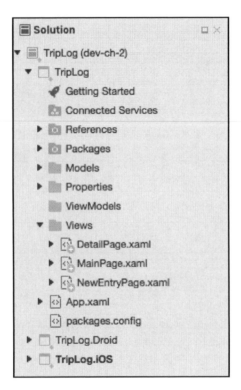

In MVVM, the term View is used to describe a screen. Xamarin.Forms uses the term View to describe controls, such as buttons or labels, and uses the term Page to describe a screen. In order to avoid confusion, I will stick with the Xamarin.Forms terminology and refer to screens as Pages, and will only use the term Views in reference to screens for the folder where the Pages will live, in order to stick with the MVVM pattern.

Adding ViewModels

In most cases, Views (Pages) and ViewModels have a one-to-one relationship. However, it is possible for a View (Page) to contain multiple ViewModels or for a ViewModel to be used by multiple Views (Pages). For now, we will simply have a single ViewModel for each Page. Before we create our ViewModels, we will start by creating a base ViewModel class, which will be an abstract class containing the basic functionality that each of our ViewModels will inherit. Initially, the base ViewModel abstract class will only contain a couple of members and wilimplement INotifyPropertyChanged, but we will add to this class as we continue to build upon the TripLog app throughout this book.

In order to create a base ViewModel, perform the following steps:

1. Create a new abstract class named BaseViewModel in the ViewModels folder using the following code:

```
public abstract class BaseViewModel
{
    protected BaseViewModel()
    {
    }
}
```

2. Update BaseViewModel to implement INotifyPropertyChanged:

```
public abstract class BaseViewModel : INotifyPropertyChanged
{
    protected BaseViewModel()
    {
    }

    public event PropertyChangedEventHandler PropertyChanged;

    protected virtual void OnPropertyChanged(
        [CallerMemberName] string propertyName = null)
    {
```

```
        PropertyChanged?.Invoke(this,
            new PropertyChangedEventArgs(propertyName));
    }
}
```

The implementation of `INotifyPropertyChanged` is key to the behavior and role of the ViewModels and data binding. It allows a Page to be notified when the properties of its ViewModel have changed.

Now that we have created a base ViewModel, we can start adding the actual ViewModels that will serve as the data context for each of our Pages. We will start by creating a ViewModel for `MainPage`.

Adding MainViewModel

The main purpose of a ViewModel is to separate the business logic, for example, data access and data manipulation, from the user interface logic. Right now, our `MainPage` directly defines the list of data that it is displaying. This data will eventually be dynamically loaded from an API but for now, we will move this initial static data definition to its ViewModel so that it can be data bound to the user interface.

In order to create the ViewModel for `MainPage`, perform the following steps:

1. Create a new class file in the `ViewModels` folder and name it `MainViewModel`.
2. Update the `MainViewModel` class to inherit from `BaseViewModel`:

```
public class MainViewModel : BaseViewModel
{
    // ...
}
```

3. Add an `ObservableCollection<T>` property to the `MainViewModel` class and name it `LogEntries`. This property will be used to bind to the `ItemsSource` property of the `ListView` element on `MainPage.xaml`:

```
public class MainViewModel : BaseViewModel
{
    ObservableCollection<TripLogEntry> _logEntries;
    public ObservableCollection<TripLogEntry> LogEntries
    {
        get { return _logEntries; }
        set
        {
            _logEntries = value;
```

```
            OnPropertyChanged ();
        }
    }

    // ...
}
```

4. Next, remove the `List<TripLogEntry>` that populates the `ListView` element on `MainPage.xaml` and repurpose that logic in the `MainViewModel`—we will put it in the constructor for now:

```csharp
public MainViewModel()
{
    LogEntries = new ObservableCollection<TripLogEntry>();

    LogEntries.Add(new TripLogEntry
    {
        Title = "Washington Monument",
        Notes = "Amazing!",
        Rating = 3,
        Date = new DateTime(2017, 2, 5),
        Latitude = 38.8895,
        Longitude = -77.0352
    });

    LogEntries.Add(new TripLogEntry
    {
        Title = "Statue of Liberty",
        Notes = "Inspiring!",
        Rating = 4,
        Date = new DateTime(2017, 4, 13),
        Latitude = 40.6892,
        Longitude = -74.0444
    });

    LogEntries.Add(new TripLogEntry
    {
        Title = "Golden Gate Bridge",
        Notes = "Foggy, but beautiful.",
        Rating = 5,
        Date = new DateTime(2017, 4, 26),
        Latitude = 37.8268,
        Longitude = -122.4798
    });
}
```

5. Set `MainViewModel` as the `BindingContext` property for `MainPage`. Do this by simply setting the `BindingContext` property of `MainPage` in its code-behind file to a new instance of `MainViewModel`. The `BindingContext` property comes from the `Xamarin.Forms.ContentPage` base class:

```
public MainPage()
{
    InitializeComponent();

    BindingContext = new MainViewModel();
}
```

6. Finally, update how the `ListView` element on `MainPage.xaml` gets its items. Currently, its `ItemsSource` property is being set directly in the Page's code behind. Remove this and instead update the `ListView` element's tag in `MainPage.xaml` to bind to the `MainViewModel LogEntries` property:

```
<ListView ... ItemsSource="{Binding LogEntries}">
```

Adding DetailViewModel

Next, we will add another ViewModel to serve as the data context for `DetailPage`, as follows:

1. Create a new class file in the `ViewModels` folder and name it `DetailViewModel`.

2. Update the `DetailViewModel` class to inherit from the `BaseViewModel` abstract class:

```
public class DetailViewModel : BaseViewModel
{
    // ...
}
```

3. Add a `TripLogEntry` property to the class and name it `Entry`. This property will be used to bind details about an entry to the various labels on `DetailPage`:

```
public class DetailViewModel : BaseViewModel
{
    TripLogEntry _entry;
    public TripLogEntry Entry
    {
        get { return _entry; }
        set
```

```
        {
            _entry = value;
            OnPropertyChanged ();
        }
    }

    // ...
}
```

4. Update the `DetailViewModel` constructor to take a `TripLogEntry` parameter named `entry`. Use this constructor property to populate the public `Entry` property created in the previous step:

```
public class DetailViewModel : BaseViewModel
{
    // ...

    public DetailViewModel(TripLogEntry entry)
    {
        Entry = entry;
    }
}
```

5. Set `DetailViewModel` as the `BindingContext` for `DetailPage` and pass in the `TripLogEntry` property that is being passed to `DetailPage`:

```
public DetailPage (TripLogEntry entry)
{
    InitializeComponent ();

    BindingContext = new DetailViewModel(entry);

    // ...
}
```

In Chapter 3, *Navigation,* we will refactor how we are passing the entry parameter to `DetailViewModel`.

6. Next, remove the code at the end of the `DetailPage` constructor that directly sets the `Text` properties of the `Label` elements:

```
public DetailPage(TripLogEntry entry)
{
    // ...
```

```
        // Remove these lines of code:
        //title.Text = entry.Title;
        //date.Text = entry.Date.ToString("M");
        //rating.Text = $"{entry.Rating} star rating";
        //notes.Text = entry.Notes;
    }
```

7. Next, update the `Label` element tags in `DetailPage.xaml` to bind their `Text` properties to the `DetailViewModel` `Entry` property:

```
<Label ... Text="{Binding Entry.Title}" />
<Label ... Text="{Binding Entry.Date, StringFormat='{0:M}'}" />
<Label ... Text="{Binding Entry.Rating, StringFormat='{0} star
rating'}" />
<Label ... Text="{Binding Entry.Notes}" />
```

8. Finally, update the map to get the values it is plotting from the ViewModel. Since the Xamarin.Forms `Map` control does not have bindable properties, the values have to be set directly to the ViewModel properties. The easiest way to do this is to add a private field to the page that returns the value of the page's `BindingContext` and then use that field to set the values on the map:

```
public partial class DetailPage : ContentPage
{
    DetailViewModel _vm
    {
        get { return BindingContext as DetailViewModel; }
    }

    public DetailPage(TripLogEntry entry)
    {
        InitializeComponent();

        BindingContext = new DetailViewModel(entry);

        TripMap.MoveToRegion(MapSpan.FromCenterAndRadius(
            new Position(_vm.Entry.Latitude, _vm.Entry.Longitude),
            Distance.FromMiles(.5)));

        TripMap.Pins.Add(new Pin
        {
            Type = PinType.Place,
            Label = _vm.Entry.Title,
            Position =
                new Position(_vm.Entry.Latitude, _vm.Entry.Longitude)
        });
```

```
            }
        }
```

Adding NewEntryViewModel

Finally, we will need to add a ViewModel for NewEntryPage, as follows:

1. Create a new class file in the ViewModels folder and name it NewEntryViewModel.

2. Update the NewEntryViewModel class to inherit from BaseViewModel:

```
public class NewEntryViewModel : BaseViewModel
{
    // ...
}
```

3. Add public properties to the NewEntryViewModel class that will be used to bind it to the values entered into the EntryCell elements in NewEntryPage.xaml:

```
public class NewEntryViewModel : BaseViewModel
{
    string _title;
    public string Title
    {
        get { return _title; }
        set
        {
            _title = value;
            OnPropertyChanged();
        }
    }

    double _latitude;
    public double Latitude
    {
        get { return _latitude; }
        set
        {
            _latitude = value;
            OnPropertyChanged();
        }
    }

    double _longitude;
    public double Longitude
```

```
    {
        get { return _longitude; }
        set
        {
            _longitude = value;
            OnPropertyChanged();
        }
    }

    DateTime _date;
    public DateTime Date
    {
        get { return _date; }
        set
        {
            _date = value;
            OnPropertyChanged();
        }
    }

    int _rating;
    public int Rating
    {
        get { return _rating; }
        set
        {
            _rating = value;
            OnPropertyChanged();
        }
    }

    string _notes;
    public string Notes
    {
        get { return _notes; }
        set
        {
            _notes = value;
            OnPropertyChanged();
        }
    }

    // ...
}
```

4. Update the `NewEntryViewModel` constructor to initialize the `Date` and `Rating` properties:

```
public NewEntryViewModel()
{
    Date = DateTime.Today;
    Rating = 1;
}
```

5. Add a public `Command` property to `NewEntryViewModel` and name it `SaveCommand`. This property will be used to bind to the **Save** `ToolbarItem` in `NewEntryPage.xaml`. The Xamarin. Forms `Command` type implements `System.Windows.Input.ICommand` to provide an `Action` to run when the command is executed, and a `Func` to determine whether the command can be executed:

```
public class NewEntryViewModel : BaseViewModel
{
    // ...

    Command _saveCommand;
    public Command SaveCommand
    {
        get
        {
            return _saveCommand ?? (_saveCommand =
                new Command(ExecuteSaveCommand, CanSave));
        }
    }

    void ExecuteSaveCommand()
    {
        var newItem = new TripLogEntry
        {
            Title = Title,
            Latitude = Latitude,
            Longitude = Longitude,
            Date = Date,
            Rating = Rating,
            Notes = Notes
        };

        // TODO: Persist Entry in a later chapter.
    }

    bool CanSave ()
```

```
    {
            return !string.IsNullOrWhiteSpace (Title);
    }
}
```

6. In order to keep the `CanExecute` function of the `SaveCommand` up to date, we will need to call the `SaveCommand.ChangeCanExecute()` method in any property setters that impact the results of that `CanExecute` function. In our case, this is only the `Title` property:

```
public string Title
{
    get { return _title; }
    set
    {
        _title = value;
        OnPropertyChanged();
        SaveCommand.ChangeCanExecute();
    }
}
```

The `CanExecute` function is not required, but by providing it, you can automatically manipulate the state of the control in the UI that is bound to the `Command` so that it is disabled until all of the required criteria are met, at which point it becomes enabled.

7. Next, set `NewEntryViewModel` as the `BindingContext` for `NewEntryPage`:

```
public NewEntryPage()
{
    InitializeComponent();

    BindingContext = new NewEntryViewModel();

    // ...
}
```

8. Next, update the `EntryCell` elements in `NewEntryPage.xaml` to bind to the `NewEntryViewModel` properties:

```
<EntryCell Label="Title" Text="{Binding Title}" />
<EntryCell Label="Latitude" Text="{Binding Latitude}" ... />
<EntryCell Label="Longitude" Text="{Binding Longitude}" ... />
<EntryCell Label="Date"
        Text="{Binding Date, StringFormat='{0:d}'}" />
```

```
<EntryCell Label="Rating" Text="{Binding Rating}" ... />
<EntryCell Label="Notes" Text="{Binding Notes}" />
```

9. Finally, we will need to update the **Save** ToolbarItem element in NewEntryPage.xaml to bind to the NewEntryViewModel SaveCommand property:

```
<ToolbarItem Text="Save" Command="{Binding SaveCommand}" />
```

Now, when we run the app and navigate to the new entry page, we can see the data binding in action, as shown in the following screenshots. Notice how the Save button is disabled until the title field contains a value:

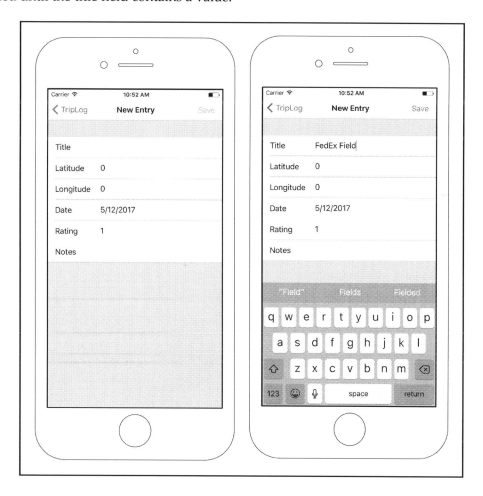

Summary

In this chapter, we updated the app that we started creating in Chapter 1, *Getting Started*, by removing data and data-related logic from the Pages, offloading it to a series of ViewModels, and then binding the Pages to those ViewModels. In the next chapter, we will expand on the Xamarin.Forms navigation service so that we can also move navigation code from the Pages to the ViewModels.

3
Navigation

The overarching goal of this book is to show how you can build a solid architecture based on design patterns and best practices; the objective of this chapter is to take our TripLog app one step closer to achieving that goal. By introducing MVVM into our TripLog app in `Chapter 2`, *MVVM and Data Binding*, we set up the app with a very clear pattern to separate the user interface from the rest of the logic in the app. Each subsequent chapter, starting with this one, further advances this concept of separation.

In `Chapter 2`, *MVVM and Data Binding*, we moved a large portion of the app logic into ViewModels; however, navigation is still being initiated from the Pages (Views). In this chapter, we will also move navigation into `ViewModels`.

Here is a quick look at what we'll cover in this chapter:

- Understanding the basics of the Xamarin.Forms navigation API
- Thinking about navigation in MVVM
- Creating a navigation service
- Updating the TripLog app to use the navigation service

The Xamarin.Forms navigation API

Along with abstracting common user interface elements into a multi-platform API, Xamarin.Forms also abstracts navigation for iOS, Android, and Windows into a single easy-to-use navigation service. Each mobile platform does navigation in a slightly different way and has a slightly different navigation API; however, at their core, they all accomplish similar tasks and in most cases use a stack structure—last in, first out.

The Xamarin.Forms navigation API uses stack-like terminology, closely resembling the navigation APIs of iOS. The Xamarin.Forms navigation API is exposed through the `Xamarin.Forms.INavigation` interface, which is implemented via the `Navigation` property that can be called from any `Xamarin.Forms.VisualElement` object, but typically `Xamarin.Forms.Page`. `Xamarin.Forms.NavigationPage` also implements the `INavigation` interface and exposes public methods to perform common navigation tasks.

The Xamarin.Forms navigation API supports two types of navigation: standard and modal. **Standard navigation** is the typical navigation pattern where the user clicks or taps through a series of pages and is able to use either device/operating system-provided functionality (back buttons on Android and Windows), or app-provided elements (navigation bar on iOS and action bar on Android), to navigate back through the stack. **Modal navigation** is similar to the modal dialog concept in web apps where a new page is layered on top of the calling page, preventing interaction with the calling page until the user performs a specific action to close the modal page. On smaller form factor devices, modal pages typically take up the entire screen, whereas on larger form factors such as tablets, modal pages may only take up a subset of the screen, more like a dialog. The `Xamarin.Forms.INavigation` interface exposes two separate read-only properties to view the standard and modal navigation stacks: `NavigationStack` and `ModalStack`.

The `Xamarin.Forms.INavigation` interface provides several methods to asynchronously push and pop pages onto the navigation and modal stacks, as follows:

- `PushAsync(Page page)` and `PushAsync(Page page, bool animated)` to navigate to a new page
- `PopAsync()` and `PopAsync(bool animated)` to navigate back to the previous page, if there is one
- `PushModalAsync(Page page)` and `PushModalAsync(Page page, bool animated)` to modally display a page
- `PopModalAsync()` and `PopModalAsync(bool animated)` to dismiss the current modally displayed page

In addition to these methods, there are also a few methods that help you manipulate the navigation stack since it is exposed as a read-only property:

- `InsertPageBefore(Page page, Page before)` to insert a page before a specific page that is already in the navigation stack
- `RemovePage(Page page)` to remove a specific page in the navigation stack
- `PopToRootAsync()` and `PopToRootAsync(bool animated)` to navigate back to the first page and remove all others in the navigation stack

We've already used `PushAsync` a few times in the TripLog app to allow the user to move from page to page. In the next couple of sections of this chapter, we'll create a custom navigation service that extends the Xamarin.Forms navigation API, use it to move those instances of `PushAsync` from the Views into the ViewModels, and expose them through commands that will be data bound to the Page.

Navigation and MVVM

One of the key purposes of the MVVM pattern is to isolate an app's presentation layer from its other layers. In doing so, an app's business logic is also isolated. One of the thoughts behind this isolation is to have a user interface that is only concerned with displaying data, and that is completely independent of how that data is stored, acquired, manipulated, or shared with the rest of the app. As explained in `Chapter 2`, *MVVM and Data Binding*, this is typically accomplished through data binding. In MVVM, the actions that a user performs on a page are bound to commands on that page's backing ViewModel. It is very common for these actions to result in a transition to another page—either by directly linking to it or by automatically navigating to a previous page after performing a task, such as saving data. Therefore, it makes sense to rethink how we implement navigation in an app that leverages the MVVM pattern so that it can be controlled by the ViewModels and not by the pages.

Most of the common third-party MVVM frameworks and toolkits subscribe to this theory and often even provide a navigation service that is designed for ViewModel consumption.

There are two main approaches to consider when performing navigation within ViewModels—one is the page-centric approach, and the other is the ViewModel-centric approach. A page-centric approach involves navigating to another page by a direct reference to that page. A ViewModel-centric approach involves navigating to another page by reference to that page's ViewModel.

The page-centric approach can be accomplished in Xamarin.Forms by simply passing the current `Xamarin.Forms.INavigation` instance into a ViewModel's constructor. From there, the ViewModel can use the default Xamarin.Forms navigation mechanism to navigate to other pages. The benefits of this approach are that it separates the navigation functionality from the page layer and is fairly quick to implement. However, the downside is that it puts a strong dependency on direct page references into ViewModels. I typically prefer to use the ViewModel-centric approach and keep ViewModels loosely coupled and unaware of the actual page implementations.

The ViewModel-centric navigation

As previously discussed, the ViewModel-centric approach alleviates a ViewModel from having any dependencies on the specific implementation of individual pages. In a default Xamarin.Forms solution, this might not appear to be such a big deal, but consider a situation where pages were self-contained in their own library—the library containing ViewModels probably wouldn't have a reference to that library. This is typical of a traditional Xamarin-based multi-platform solution architecture and also a good practice to follow.

Since a ViewModel doesn't navigate directly to a page, it will navigate to a page via the page's ViewModel. This means that when implementing this approach, there is a need to build a relationship, or mapping, between pages and their ViewModels. As with most things in software development, this can be done in a couple of ways. One way is to include a dictionary or key-value type property in the navigation service that maintains a one-to-one mapping of pages and ViewModels using their type. This could also be done externally to the navigation service to provide an additional abstraction. Another approach employed by the **MVVM Light** (http://www.mvvmlight.net/) toolkit's navigation service is to map the type of ViewModel with a `string` key that represents the actual page it relates to.

In the next section, we'll create a ViewModel-centric navigation service that includes ViewModel and page type mapping.

Creating a navigation service

In a typical multi-platform mobile app architecture, one would have to implement a platform-specific navigation service for each platform the app supports. In our case, Xamarin.Forms has already done this, so we will simply implement a single navigation service that extends the Xamarin.Forms navigation abstraction so that we can perform ViewModel-to-ViewModel navigation.

The first thing we will need to do is define an interface for our navigation service that will define its methods. We will start with an interface so that the service can be added to ViewModels via constructor injection, which we'll dive into in `Chapter 4`, *Platform-Specific Services and Dependency Injection,* and we can easily provide alternative implementations of the service without changing ViewModels that depend on it. A common scenario for this is creating a mock of the service that gets used when unit testing ViewModels.

In order to create the navigation service, perform the following steps:

1. Create a new `Services` folder in the core library.
2. Create a new interface named `INavService` with the following methods:

```
public interface INavService
{
    bool CanGoBack { get; }
    Task GoBack();
    Task NavigateTo<TVM>()
        where TVM : BaseViewModel;
    Task NavigateTo<TVM, TParameter>(TParameter parameter)
        where TVM : BaseViewModel;
    Task RemoveLastView();
    Task ClearBackStack();
    Task NavigateToUri(Uri uri);

    event PropertyChangedEventHandler CanGoBackChanged;
}
```

This interface defines fairly standard navigation behavior—the ability to navigate to ViewModels, navigate back, clear the navigation stack, and navigate to a regular URI. The `NavigateTo` method defines a generic type and restricts its use to objects of the `BaseViewModel` base class, which we created in the previous chapter. There is also an overloaded `NavigateTo` method that enables a strongly typed parameter to be passed along with the navigation.

Before we create the actual implementation of the `INavService` interface, we will need to make a couple of updates to our `BaseViewModel`:

1. Update the `BaseViewModel` to include an abstract `Init` method:

```
public abstract class BaseViewModel
{
    // ...
```

```
        public abstract Task Init();
}
```

2. Next, add a second `BaseViewModel` abstract base class with a generic type that will be used to pass strongly typed parameters to the `Init` method:

```
public abstract class BaseViewModel<TParameter> : BaseViewModel
{
    protected BaseViewModel() : base()
    {
    }

    public override async Task Init()
    {
        await Init (default(TParameter));
    }

    public abstract Task Init (TParameter parameter);
}
```

3. Then, update `MainViewModel` and `NewEntryViewModel` to override the `Init` method. For now, the `NewEntryViewModel Init` method will just be a blank implementation. The `Init` method in `MainViewModel` will be responsible for loading the log entries. We will move the log entry list population logic out of the constructor and into a new `async` method named `LoadEntries`, which will be called from the `Init` override:

```
public MainViewModel() : base()
{
    LogEntries = new ObservableCollection<TripLogEntry>();
}

public override async Task Init()
{
    await LoadEntries();
}

async Task LoadEntries()
{
    LogEntries.Clear();

    await Task.Factory.StartNew(() =>
    {
        LogEntries.Add(new TripLogEntry
        {
            Title = "Washington Monument",
```

```
            Notes = "Amazing!",
            Rating = 3,
            Date = new DateTime(2017, 2, 5),
            Latitude = 38.8895,
            Longitude = -77.0352
        });

        LogEntries.Add(new TripLogEntry
        {
            Title = "Statue of Liberty",
            Notes = "Inspiring!",
            Rating = 4,
            Date = new DateTime(2017, 4, 13),
            Latitude = 40.6892,
            Longitude = -74.0444
        });

        LogEntries.Add(new TripLogEntry
        {
            Title = "Golden Gate Bridge",
            Notes = "Foggy, but beautiful.",
            Rating = 5,
            Date = new DateTime(2017, 4, 26),
            Latitude = 37.8268,
            Longitude = -122.4798
        });
    });
}
```

4. Next, update `DetailViewModel` to inherit from `BaseViewModel<TripLogEntry>` and override the `Init` method, and set the `Entry` property with the value of its `TripLogEntry` parameter:

```
public class DetailViewModel : BaseViewModel<TripLogEntry>
{
    // ...

    public DetailViewModel() // <- Remove parameter
    {
    }

    public override async Task Init(TripLogEntry logEntry)
    {
        Entry = logEntry;
    }
}
```

Note that because we are setting the `Entry` property within the `Init` method, we can now remove the `TripLogEntry` parameter from the constructor.

5. We will also need to remove the `TripLogEntry` parameter from the `DetailPage` constructor as it will now all be handled between the navigation service and the ViewModel's `Init` method:

```
public class DetailPage : ContentPage
{
    // ...

    public DetailPage() // <- Remove parameter
    {
        InitializeComponent();

        BindingContext = new DetailViewModel();

        // ...
    }
}
```

Now that `BaseViewModel` has been updated, we can create our navigation service that implements `INavService`.

1. Create a new class within the `Services` folder of the core library. Name the new class `XamarinFormsNavService` and make it implement `INavService` as follows:

```
public class XamarinFormsNavService : INavService
{
}
```

2. Update the `XamarinFormsNavService` to include a public `INavigation` property named `XamarinFormsNav`. This `XamarinFormsNav` property provides a reference to the current `Xamarin.Forms.INavigation` instance and will need to be set when the navigation service is first initialized, which we'll see later in this section when we update the TripLog app:

```
public class XamarinFormsNavService : INavService
{
    public INavigation XamarinFormsNav { get; set; }

    // TODO: INavService implementation goes here.
}
```

As discussed in the previous section, we will implement the navigation service with a page-to-ViewModel mapping. We will do this with an IDictionary<Type, Type> property and a method to register the mappings.

3. Update the XamarinFormsNavService with an IDictionary<Type, Type> read-only property and add a public method named RegisterViewMapping to populate it:

```
public class XamarinFormsNavService : INavService
{
    readonly IDictionary<Type, Type> _map = new Dictionary<Type,
Type>();

    public void RegisterViewMapping(Type viewModel, Type view)
    {
        _map.Add(viewModel, view);
    }

    // ...

}
```

4. Next, implement the INavService methods. Most of the INavService methods will leverage the XamarinFormNav property to make calls to the Xamarin.Forms navigation API in order to perform the navigation and alter the navigation stack:

```
public class XamarinFormsNavService : INavService
{
    // ...

    public bool CanGoBack
    {
        get
        {
            return XamarinFormsNav.NavigationStack != null
                && XamarinFormsNav.NavigationStack.Count > 0;
        }
    }

    public async Task GoBack()
    {
        if (CanGoBack)
        {
            await XamarinFormsNav.PopAsync(true);
        }
```

```
        OnCanGoBackChanged();
    }

    public async Task NavigateTo<TVM>() where TVM : BaseViewModel
    {
        await NavigateToView(typeof(TVM));

        if (XamarinFormsNav.NavigationStack.Last().BindingContext is
BaseViewModel)
        {
            await ((BaseViewModel)(XamarinFormsNav
                .NavigationStack.Last().BindingContext)).Init();
        }
    }

    public async Task NavigateTo<TVM, TParameter>(TParameter
parameter)
        where TVM : BaseViewModel
    {
        await NavigateToView(typeof(TVM));
        if (XamarinFormsNav.NavigationStack.Last().BindingContext is
BaseViewModel<TParameter>)
        {
            await ((BaseViewModel<TParameter>)(XamarinFormsNav
.NavigationStack.Last().BindingContext)).Init(parameter);
        }
    }

    async Task NavigateToView(Type viewModelType)
    {
        Type viewType;

        if (!_map.TryGetValue(viewModelType, out viewType))
        {
            throw new ArgumentException("No view found in View
Mapping for " + viewModelType.FullName + ".");
        }

        var constructor = viewType.GetTypeInfo()
                                   .DeclaredConstructors
                                   .FirstOrDefault(dc =>
dc.GetParameters().Count() <= 0);

        var view = constructor.Invoke(null) as Page;
        await XamarinFormsNav.PushAsync(view, true);
    }

    public async Task RemoveLastView()
```

```
            {
                if (XamarinFormsNav.NavigationStack.Any())
                {
                    var lastView = XamarinFormsNav
.NavigationStack[XamarinFormsNav.NavigationStack.Count - 2];
                    XamarinFormsNav.RemovePage(lastView);
                }
            }

            public async Task ClearBackStack()
            {
                if (XamarinFormsNav.NavigationStack.Count <= 1)
                {
                    return;
                }

                for (var i = 0; i < XamarinFormsNav.NavigationStack.Count -
1; i++)
                {
XamarinFormsNav.RemovePage(XamarinFormsNav.NavigationStack[i]);
                }
            }

            public async Task NavigateToUri(Uri uri)
            {
                if (uri == null)
                {
                    throw new ArgumentException("Invalid URI");
                }

                Device.OpenUri(uri);
            }

            public event PropertyChangedEventHandler CanGoBackChanged;

            void OnCanGoBackChanged()
            {
                CanGoBackChanged?.Invoke(this, new
                    PropertyChangedEventArgs("CanGoBack"));
            }
        }
```

5. Finally, the navigation service class needs to be marked as a dependency so that it can be resolved by the Xamarin.Forms DependencyService. This is accomplished by adding an `assembly` attribute to the class before the namespace block, as shown in the following code:

```
[assembly: Dependency(typeof(XamarinFormsNavService))]
namespace TripLog.Services
{
    public class XamarinFormsNavService : INavService
    {
        // ...
    }
}
```

In Chapter 4, *Platform-Specific Services and Dependency Injection*, we will remove this as we replace the Xamarin.Forms DependencyService with a third-party dependency injection library.

Updating the TripLog app

With the navigation service completed, we can now update the rest of the TripLog app to leverage it. To start with, we will update the constructor in the main `App` class in `App.xaml.cs` to create a new instance of the navigation service and register the app's page-to-ViewModel mappings:

```
public App()
{
    var mainPage = new NavigationPage(new MainPage());
    var navService = DependencyService.Get<INavService>() as
XamarinFormsNavService;

    navService.XamarinFormsNav = mainPage.Navigation;

    navService.RegisterViewMapping(typeof(MainViewModel),
                                    typeof(MainPage));
    navService.RegisterViewMapping(typeof(DetailViewModel),
                                    typeof(DetailPage));
    navService.RegisterViewMapping(typeof(NewEntryViewModel),
                                    typeof(NewEntryPage));

    MainPage = mainPage;
}
```

Updating BaseViewModel

Since most ViewModels in the TripLog app will need to use the navigation service, it makes sense to include it in the `BaseViewModel` class:

```
public abstract class BaseViewModel : INotifyPropertyChanged
{
    protected INavService NavService { get; private set; }

    protected BaseViewModel(INavService navService)
    {
        NavService = navService;
    }

    // ...
}
```

Each of the ViewModels that inherit from `BaseViewModel` will need to be updated to include an `INavService` parameter in their constructors that is then passed to its `BaseViewModel` base class. The `BaseViewModel<TParameter>` base class needs to be updated to include an `INavService` constructor parameter as well.

In addition, each ViewModel initialization needs to be updated to pass in an `INavService`, which can be retrieved from the Xamarin.Forms DependencyService:

1. Update the `MainViewModel` instantiation in the `MainPage` constructor:

```
public MainPage()
{
    BindingContext = new
MainViewModel(DependencyService.Get<INavService>());
    // ...
}
```

2. Update the `DetailViewModel` instantiation in the `DetailPage` constructor:

```
public DetailPage()
{
    BindingContext = new
DetailViewModel(DependencyService.Get<INavService>());

    // ...
}
```

3. Update the `NewEntryViewModel` instantiation in the `NewEntryPage` constructor:

```
public NewEntryPage()
{
    BindingContext = new
NewEntryViewModel(DependencyService.Get<INavService>());

    // ...
}
```

Updating MainViewModel

In order to move the navigation functionality from `MainPage` to `MainViewModel`, we will need to add two new `Command` properties—one for creating a new log entry and another for viewing the details of an existing log entry:

```
public class MainViewModel : BaseViewModel
{
    // ...

    Command<TripLogEntry> _viewCommand;
    public Command<TripLogEntry> ViewCommand
    {
        get
        {
            return _viewCommand
                ?? (_viewCommand = new Command<TripLogEntry>(async
(entry) => await ExecuteViewCommand(entry)));
        }
    }

    Command _newCommand;
    public Command NewCommand
    {
        get
        {
            return _newCommand
                ?? (_newCommand = new Command(async () => await
ExecuteNewCommand()));
        }
    }

    async Task ExecuteViewCommand(TripLogEntry entry)
    {
        await NavService.NavigateTo<DetailViewModel,
TripLogEntry>(entry);
```

```
    }

    async Task ExecuteNewCommand()
    {
        await NavService.NavigateTo<NewEntryViewModel>();
    }

    // ...
}
```

With the `Command` properties in place on `MainViewModel`, we can now update `MainPage` to use these commands instead of using the Xamarin.Forms navigation service directly from the page:

1. Create a private `MainViewModel` property named _vm in the `MainPage` class that simply provides access to the page's `BindingContext`, but is casted as a `MainViewModel`:

```
public class MainPage : ContentPage
{
    MainViewModel _vm
    {
        get { return BindingContext as MainViewModel; }
    }

    // ...
}
```

2. Replace the `Navigation.PushAsync` method call in the `ItemTapped` event handler for the entries `ListView` with a call to the `ViewCommand`:

```
void Trips_ItemTapped(object sender, ItemTappedEventArgs e)
{
    var trip = (TripLogEntry)e.Item;
    _vm.ViewCommand.Execute(trip);

    trips.SelectedItem = null;
};
```

3. Replace the `Clicked` attribute on the **New** `ToolbarItem` element with a `Command` attribute whose value is a binding to the `NewCommand`:

```
<ToolbarItem Text="New" Command="{Binding NewCommand}" />
```

Initializing MainViewModel

The `XamarinFormsNavService` custom navigation service we created handles initializing ViewModels automatically when they are navigated to by calling the `Init` method in `BaseViewModel`. However, because the main page is launched by default and not via navigation, we will need to manually call the `Init` method on the page's ViewModel when the page first appears.

Update `MainPage` by overriding its `OnAppearing` method to call its ViewModel's `Init` method:

```
public class MainPage : ContentPage
{
    // ...
    protected override async void OnAppearing()
    {
        base.OnAppearing ();

        // Initialize MainViewModel
        if (_vm != null)
            await _vm.Init();
    }
}
```

Updating NewEntryViewModel

In Chapter 2, *MVVM and Data Binding*, we added `SaveCommand` to `NewEntryViewModel`, but once the `SaveCommand` executed, nothing occurred. Once `SaveCommand` performs its logic to save the new log entry, it should navigate the user back to the previous page. We can accomplish this by updating the execute `Action` of `SaveCommand` to call the `GoBack` method in the navigation service that we created in the last section:

```
public class NewEntryViewModel : BaseViewModel
{
    // ...

    Command _saveCommand;
    public Command SaveCommand
    {
        get
        {
            return _saveCommand
                ?? (_saveCommand = new Command(async () => await
ExecuteSaveCommand(), CanSave));
        }
```

```
    }

    // ...

    async Task ExecuteSaveCommand()
    {
        var newItem = new TripLogEntry
        {
            Title = Title,
            Latitude = Latitude,
            Longitude = Longitude,
            Date = Date,
            Rating = Rating,
            Notes = Notes
        };

        // TODO: Persist Entry in a later chapter.

        await NavService.GoBack();
    }
}
```

Notice that because the `ExecuteSaveCommand` method now calls an asynchronous method, it needs to use `async` and `await`, and its return type needs to be updated from `void` to `Task`.

Updating DetailPage

Finally, we will need to update how the map on `DetailPage` is being bound to the data in the `DetailViewModel`. Since the ViewModel is being initialized via the navigation service now, it happens after the page is constructed, and therefore the map doesn't have the data it needs. Normally, this would not be a problem thanks to data binding; however, since the map control does not allow for data binding, we will need to handle its data differently. The best way for the page to check when its ViewModel has data for its map control is to handle the ViewModel's `PropertyChanged` event. If the ViewModel's `Entry` property changes, the map control should be updated accordingly, as shown in the following steps:

1. First, move the two statements that plot and center the coordinates on the map control out of the constructor and into a separate private method named `UpdateMap` in the `DetailPage` class:

```
public partial class DetailPage : ContentPage
{
    // ...
```

```
            public DetailPage()
            {
                InitializeComponent();

                BindingContext = new
    DetailViewModel(DependencyService.Get<INavService>());
            }

            void UpdateMap()
            {
                if (_vm.Entry == null)
                {
                    return;
                }

                // Center the map around the log entry's location
                map.MoveToRegion(MapSpan.FromCenterAndRadius(
                    new Position(_vm.Entry.Latitude,
                                 _vm.Entry.Longitude),
                                 Distance.FromMiles(.5)));

                // Place a pin on the map for the log entry's location
                map.Pins.Add(new Pin
                {
                    Type = PinType.Place,
                    Label = _vm.Entry.Title,
                    Position = new Position(_vm.Entry.Latitude,
    _vm.Entry.Longitude)
                });
            }
        }
```

2. Next, handle the ViewModel's `PropertyChanged` event to update the map when the ViewModel's `Entry` property is changed:

```
public partial class DetailPage : ContentPage
{
    // ...

    public DetailPage()
    {
        // ...
    }

    void UpdateMap()
    {
```

```
            // ...
        }

    void OnViewModelPropertyChanged(object sender,
PropertyChangedEventArgs args)
        {
            if (args.PropertyName == nameof(DetailViewModel.Entry))
            {
                UpdateMap();
            }
        }

    protected override void OnAppearing()
        {
            base.OnAppearing();

            if (_vm != null)
            {
                _vm.PropertyChanged += OnViewModelPropertyChanged;
            }
        }

    protected override void OnDisappearing()
        {
            base.OnDisappearing();

            if (_vm != null)
            {
                _vm.PropertyChanged -= OnViewModelPropertyChanged;
            }
        }
    }
```

Summary

In this chapter, we created a service that extends the default Xamarin.Forms navigation API to enable a ViewModel-centric navigation, enforcing a better separation between the presentation layer and the business logic in ViewModels.

In Chapter 4, *Platform-Specific Services and Dependency Injection*, we will create some additional services that abstract platform-specific APIs and replace the Xamarin.Forms DependencyService with a more flexible IoC and dependency injection alternative.

4

Platform Specific Services and Dependency Injection

This chapter will not teach you everything there is to know about inversion of control (IoC) and dependency injection, as there are numerous resources available that strictly focus on these topics alone. Instead, this chapter will focus on how these patterns apply to mobile development and, more specifically, how to implement them in a Xamarin.Forms mobile app.

The following is a quick look at what we'll cover in this chapter:

- The need for dependency injection in a multi-platform mobile app development
- Implementing IoC and dependency injection using a third-party library in place of Xamarin.Forms DependencyService
- Creating, injecting, and using platform-specific services
- Updating our TripLog app to use platform-specific services through dependency injection

Inversion of control and dependency injection in mobile apps

In software development, IoC and dependency injection solve many problems. In the world of mobile development, particularly multi-platform mobile development, they provide a great pattern to handle platform- and device-specific code. One of the most important aspects of multi-platform mobile development is the idea of sharing code. Not only does development become easier and quicker when code can be shared across apps and platforms, but so does maintenance, management, feature parity, and so on. However, there are always parts of an app's code base that simply cannot be shared due to its strict tie-in with the platform's APIs. In most cases, an app's user interface represents a large portion of this non-sharable code. It is because of this that the MVVM pattern makes so much sense in multi-platform mobile development—it forces the separation of user interface code (Views) into individual, platform-specific, libraries, making it easy to then compartmentalize the rest of the code (ViewModels and Models) into a single, shareable library.

However, what if the code in the shared ViewModels needs to access the device's physical geolocation, or leverage the device's camera to take a photo? Since the ViewModels exist in a single platform-agnostic library, they can't call the platform-specific APIs. This is where dependency injection saves the day.

Xamarin.Forms DependencyService versus third-party alternatives

In addition to providing the core building blocks for the MVVM pattern, Xamarin.Forms also includes a very basic service that handles dependency registration and resolution, called the DependencyService. We actually used this service in the previous chapter to register and resolve our custom navigation service. Like many of the services and components built into the Xamarin.Forms toolkit, DependencyService is designed to help get developers up and running quickly by providing an easy-to-use basic implementation. It is in no way the only way of handling dependencies in a Xamarin.Forms mobile app and, in most complex apps, you will quickly outgrow the capabilities of the Xamarin.Forms DependencyService. For example, the Xamarin.Forms DependencyService doesn't provide a way of doing constructor injection.

There are several third-party alternatives to the DependencyService that allow much greater flexibility, such as Autofac, TinyIoC, Ninject, and Unity. Each of these libraries are open sourced and, in most cases, community maintained. They all implement the patterns in slightly different ways and offer different benefits depending on the architecture of your app.

In the next couple of sections, we will build two new platform-specific services, and use the Ninject library to register and use them in our TripLog app. We will also update the navigation service from Chapter 3, *Navigation*, to be registered in Ninject, instead of the Xamarin.Forms DependencyService.

Creating and using platform-specific services

We have already created a service to handle navigation in the previous chapter. That custom navigation service specification was provided by the INavService interface and there is a property of that interface type in the BaseViewModel so that a concrete implementation of the service can be provided to the ViewModels as needed.

The benefit of using an interface to define platform-specific or third-party dependency services is that it can be used in an agnostic way in the ViewModels, and the concrete implementations can be provided via dependency injection. Those concrete implementations can be actual services, or even mocked services for unit testing the ViewModels, as we'll see in Chapter 8, *Testing*.

In addition to navigation, there are a couple of other platform-specific services our TripLog app could use to enrich its data and experience. In this section, we will create a location service that allows us to get specific geo-coordinates from the device. The actual platform-specific implementation of the location service is fairly trivial, and there are tons of resources on how to do this. We will create a basic implementation without going too deep, so that we can keep the focus on how we leverage it as a dependency in a Xamarin.Forms architecture.

Similar to the approach taken for the navigation service, we will first start out by creating an interface for the location service, and then create the actual platform-specific implementations.

Creating a location service

The first step to allowing our app to take advantage of the device's geolocation capabilities, is to provide an interface in the core library that can be used by the ViewModels in a device- and platform-agnostic manner. When receiving the geolocation back from a device, each platform could potentially provide coordinates in a platform-specific data structure. However, each structure will ultimately provide two `double` values representing the coordinate's latitude and longitude.

There are a couple of ways to ensure that the results are returned in a platform-agnostic manner, which we will need since we are working in a non-platform-specific library.

One way to ensure this is to pass the values back via a callback method. Another approach we will be employing is to use a custom object, which we will define in our `Models` namespace, as shown in the following steps:

1. Create a new class named `GeoCoords` in the `Models` folder of the core library.

2. Add two `double` properties to the `GeoCoords` class named `Latitude` and `Longitude`:

```
public class GeoCoords
{
    public double Latitude { get; set; }
    public double Longitude { get; set; }
}
```

3. Create a new interface named `ILocationService` in the `Services` folder of the core library. The interface should have one async method, which returns `Task<GeoCoords>`:

```
public interface ILocationService
{
    Task<GeoCoords> GetGeoCoordinatesAsync();
}
```

Using the location service on the new entry page

Now that we have an interface that defines our location service, we can use it in the core project of our TripLog app. The main place we will need to capture location in the app is on the new entry page, so coordinates can be attached to log entries when they are added. Since we want to keep our app logic separate from the user interface, we will use the location service in the new entry page's ViewModel, and not on the page itself.

In order to use the ILocationService interface in the NewEntryViewModel, perform the following steps:

1. First, add a read-only property to the NewEntryViewModel to hold an instance of the location service:

```
public class NewEntryViewModel : BaseViewModel
{
    readonly ILocationService _locService;

    // ...
}
```

2. Next, update the NewEntryViewModel constructor to take an ILocationService instance, and set its read-only ILocationService property:

```
public NewEntryViewModel(INavService navService,
                         ILocationService locService)
    : base(navService)
{
    _locService = locService;
    Date = DateTime.Today;
    Rating = 1;
}
```

3. Finally, update the NewEntryViewModel Init() method to use the location service to set the Latitude and Longitude double properties:

```
public override async Task Init()
{
    var coords = await _locService.GetGeoCoordinatesAsync();
    Latitude = coords.Latitude;
    Longitude = coords.Longitude;
}
```

Notice how we can completely work with the location service in the ViewModel, even though we haven't actually written the platform-specific implementation. Although, if we were to run the app, we would get a runtime error because the implementation doesn't actually exist, but it's useful to be able to work with the service through abstraction to fully build out and test the ViewModel.

Adding the location service implementation

Now that we have created an interface for our location service and updated the ViewModel, we will need to create the concrete platform-specific implementations. Create the location service implementations as follows:

1. First, create a new folder in the TripLog.iOS project named `Services`.

2. Next, create a new class file in the `Services` folder named `LocationService` that implements the `ILocationService` interface we created earlier in the chapter:

```
public class LocationService : ILocationService
{
    CLLocationManager _manager;
    TaskCompletionSource<CLLocation> _tcs;

    public async Task<GeoCoords> GetGeoCoordinatesAsync()
    {
        _manager = new CLLocationManager();
        _tcs = new TaskCompletionSource<CLLocation>();

        if (UIDevice.CurrentDevice.CheckSystemVersion(8, 0))
        {
            _manager.RequestWhenInUseAuthorization();
        }

        _manager.LocationsUpdated += (s, e) =>
        {
            _tcs.TrySetResult(e.Locations[0]);
        };

        _manager.StartUpdatingLocation();

        var location = await _tcs.Task;

        return new GeoCoords
        {
            Latitude = location.Coordinate.Latitude,
            Longitude = location.Coordinate.Longitude
        };
    }
}
```

3. Next, create a new folder in the TripLog.Droid project named `Services`.

4. Finally, create a new class file in the `Services` folder named `LocationService` that implements the `ILocationService` interface for Android:

```
public class LocationService
    : Java.Lang.Object, ILocationService, ILocationListener
{
    TaskCompletionSource<Location> _tcs;

    public async Task<GeoCoords> GetGeoCoordinatesAsync()
    {
        var manager = (LocationManager)Forms.Context
            .GetSystemService(Context.LocationService);

        _tcs = new TaskCompletionSource<Location>();

        manager.RequestSingleUpdate("gps", this, null);

        var location = await _tcs.Task;

        return new GeoCoords
        {
            Latitude = location.Latitude,
            Longitude = location.Longitude
        };
    }

    public void OnLocationChanged(Location location)
    {
        _tcs.TrySetResult(location);
    }

    public void OnProviderDisabled(string provider)
    {
    }

    public void OnProviderEnabled(string provider)
    {
    }

    public void OnStatusChanged(string provider,
        [GeneratedEnum] Availability status, Bundle extras)
    {
    }
}
```

These are extremely over-simplified location service implementations. Most real-world scenarios will require more logic, however, for the purposes of demonstrating platform-specific service dependency injection, this implementation will suffice.

> On iOS 8.0 and higher versions, you must enable location requests in the application's Info.plist. On Android, you must require ACCESS_COARSE_LOCATION or ACCESS_FINE_LOCATION permission in the application's AndroidManifest.xml

Now that we have created a platform-dependent service, it is time to register it into an IoC container so that we can use it throughout the rest of the code. In the next section, we will use Ninject to create registrations between both our location service interface and the actual platform-specific implementations. We will also update the custom navigation service that we created in Chapter 3, *Navigation*, to use Ninject in place of the default Xamarin.Forms DependencyService.

> Xamarin, along with the help of the Xamarin developer community, has developed a repository of *Plugins for Xamarin* which provide easy to use APIs for some of the most common platform-specific scenarios, including geolocation. To learn more about *Plugins for Xamarin*, visit www.github.com/xamarin/plugins.

Registering dependencies

As mentioned earlier, each dependency injection library implements the pattern slightly differently. In this section, we will use Ninject to start adding dependency injection capabilities to our TripLog app. Ninject allows you to create **Modules**, which are responsible for adding services to the IoC container. The modules are then added to a Kernel that is used to resolve the services in other areas of the app.

You can create a single Ninject module or many, depending on how your app is structured and how you want to organize your services. For the TripLog app, we will have a Ninject Module in each platform project, which is responsible for registering that platform's specific service implementations. We will also create a Ninject module in the core library, which will be responsible for registering dependencies that live in the core library, such as ViewModels and data access services, which we will add later in Chapter 6, *API Data Access*, when we start working with live data.

Registering the platform-service implementations

We will start by creating Ninject Modules in each of the platform projects, which will be responsible for registering their respective platform's specific service implementations, as shown in the following steps:

1. Add the **Portable.Ninject** NuGet package to each of the platform-specific projects.

2. Next, create a new folder in the TripLog.iOS project named `Modules`.

3. Create a new class in the Modules folder named `TripLogPlatformModule` that inherits from `Ninject.Modules.NinjectModule`:

```
public class TripLogPlatformModule : NinjectModule
{
    // ...
}
```

4. Override the `Load` method of the `NinjectModule` class and use the Ninject `Bind` method to register the iOS-specific implementation of `ILocationService` as a singleton:

```
public class TripLogPlatformModule : NinjectModule
{
    public override void Load()
    {
        Bind<ILocationService>()
            .To<LocationService>()
            .InSingletonScope();
    }
}
```

5. Next, create a folder in the TripLog.Droid project named `Modules`, then create a new class named `TripLogPlatformModule` within it that inherits from `Ninject.Modules.NinjectModule`:

```
public class TripLogPlatformModule : NinjectModule
{
    // ...
}
```

6. Finally, override the `Load` method of the `NinjectModule` class and use the Ninject `Bind` method to register the Android-specific implementation of `ILocationService` as a singleton:

```
public class TripLogPlatformModule : NinjectModule
{
    public override void Load()
    {
        Bind<ILocationService>()
            .To<LocationService>()
            .InSingletonScope();
    }
}
```

Registering the ViewModels

We can also use our IoC container to hold our ViewModels. It is a slightly different model than the one used to register the concrete implementations of our service interfaces—instead of mapping them to an interface, we will simply register them to themselves.

Since our ViewModels are in our core library, we will create another Ninject Module in the core library that will register them, as shown in the following steps:

1. Add the **Portable.Ninject** NuGet package to the core project.
2. Create a new folder in the core project named `Modules`.
3. Create a new class in the core project `Modules` folder named `TripLogCoreModule` that inherits from `Ninject.Modules.NinjectModule`:

```
public class TripLogCoreModule : NinjectModule
{
    // ...
}
```

4. Override the `Load` method of the `NinjectModule` class, and use the Ninject `Bind` method to register each of the ViewModels:

```
public class TripLogCoreModule : NinjectModule
{
    public override void Load()
    {
        // ViewModels
        Bind<MainViewModel>().ToSelf();
```

```
    Bind<DetailViewModel>().ToSelf();
    Bind<NewEntryViewModel>().ToSelf();
  }
}
```

Registering the navigation service

In the previous chapter, we created a custom navigation service and used the Xamarin.Forms DependencyService to register and resolve the navigation service. Now that we have introduced Ninject, we can swap Xamarin.Forms DependencyService out for a Ninject Module instead, in order to register the navigation service so that it can be resolved and used just like our platform-specific services.

1. First, remove the `assembly` attribute that was originally added above the class's namespace:

    ```
    // Remove assembly attribute
    // [assembly: Dependency(typeof(XamarinFormsNavService))]
    public class XamarinFormsNavService : INavService
    {
        // ...
    }
    ```

    We originally instantiated the navigation service and registered view mappings within the core App class. We can now move all of that logic into a new Ninject module. However, in order for us to instantiate our navigation service, we will require an instance of `Xamarin.Forms.INavigation`, so we will have to set this new Module up to take that in as a constructor parameter, and then its overridden `Load` method will handle creating the service, creating the view mappings, and then registering the service into the IoC container.

2. Create a new class in the core project's `Modules` folder named `TripLogNavModule` that inherits from `NinjectModule`:

    ```
    public class TripLogNavModule : NinjectModule
    {
        // ...
    }
    ```

3. Update the constructor of the `TripLogNavModule` to take in a `Xamarin.Forms.INavigation` parameter:

    ```
    public class TripLogNavModule : NinjectModule
    ```

```
{
    readonly INavigation _xfNav;

    public TripLogNavModule(INavigation xamarinFormsNavigation)
    {
        _xfNav = xamarinFormsNavigation;
    }
}
```

4. Override the `Load` method of the `NinjectModule` class to instantiate a new `XamarinFormsNavService` object:

```
public class TripLogNavModule : NinjectModule
{
    // ...

    public override void Load()
    {
        var navService = new XamarinFormsNavService();
        navService.XamarinFormsNav = _xfNav;
    }
}
```

5. Remove the ViewModel-to-View mappings from the `App` class and place them in the `TripLogNavModule.Load` override method:

```
public override void Load()
{
    var navService = new XamarinFormsNavService();
    navService.XamarinFormsNav = _xfNav;

    // Register view mappings
    navService.RegisterViewMapping(
        typeof(MainViewModel), typeof(MainPage));

    navService.RegisterViewMapping(
        typeof(DetailViewModel), typeof(DetailPage));

    navService.RegisterViewMapping(
        typeof(NewEntryViewModel), typeof(NewEntryPage));
}
```

6. Finally, update the `TripLogNavModule.Load` override method to use the Ninject `Bind` method to register the `XamarinFormsNavService` as a singleton:

```
public override void Load()
```

```
{
    var navService = new XamarinFormsNavService();
    navService.XamarinFormsNav = _xfNav;

    // Register view mappings
    navService.RegisterViewMapping(
        typeof(MainViewModel), typeof(MainPage));

    navService.RegisterViewMapping(
        typeof(DetailViewModel), typeof(DetailPage));

    navService.RegisterViewMapping(
        typeof(NewEntryViewModel), typeof(NewEntryPage));

    Bind<INavService>()
        .ToMethod(x => navService)
        .InSingletonScope();
}
```

 Platform-specific services are good candidates for singleton objects.
ViewModels can be singletons, but typically should not be.

Updating the TripLog app

Now that our platform services, navigation service, and ViewModels have all been registered in the IoC container, we will need to add the Ninject Modules that we created to the Ninject Kernel. We will do this in our main `Xamarin.Forms.Application` class: `App`.

In order to get our platform modules into the `App` class, which is in our core library, we will simply update the `App` constructor to take in `INinjectModule` parameters. Then, each platform-specific project will be responsible for passing in its respective Ninject Module when it loads the `App` at startup, as shown in the following steps:

1. Update the `App` constructor to take in `INinjectModule` parameters:

```
public App (params INinjectModule[] platformModules)
{
    // ...
}
```

2. Next, add a public `IKernel` property named Kernel to the `App` class:

```
public partial class App : Application
{
    public IKernel Kernel { get; set; }

    // ...
}
```

3. Next, update the body of the `App` constructor. In the previous section, we moved the bulk of the existing `App` constructor logic into the navigation Ninject Module. Now, the `App` constructor should only be responsible for creating the main page and initializing the Ninject Kernel with the various modules that we have created:

```
public App (params INinjectModule[] platformModules)
{
    var mainPage = new NavigationPage(new MainPage());

    // Register core services
    Kernel = new StandardKernel(
        new TripLogCoreModule(),
        new TripLogNavModule(mainPage.Navigation));

    // Register platform specific services
    Kernel.Load(platformModules);

    // Get the MainViewModel from the IoC
    mainPage.BindingContext = Kernel.Get<MainViewModel>();

    MainPage = mainPage;
}
```

Notice how we get an instance of the `MainViewModel` from the IoC container and use it to set the ViewModel of the `MainPage`. In the next section, we'll update the navigation service to do this every time we navigate to the other pages in the app.

4. Next, we will need to update the `App` instantiation in the `AppDelegate` class of our iOS project to pass in a new instance of `TripLog.iOS.Modules.TripLogPlatformModule`:

```
LoadApplication(new App(new TripLogPlatformModule()));
```

5. Finally, repeat the previous step in the `MainActivity` class of the Android project to pass in an Android platform specific Ninject Module instance to the `App` constructor.

Updating the navigation service to handle ViewModel creation and dependency injection

Currently, in the TripLog app, each page is responsible for creating its own ViewModel instance. However, because we provide a ViewModel's dependencies through its constructor, we would have to manually resolve each dependency within the `Page` class and then pass them into the ViewModel instantiation. Not only is this going to be messy code, it is also difficult to maintain, and doesn't promote loose coupling. Since we have registered our ViewModels in our IoC container, we can completely remove the ViewModel instantiations from our Pages and set our navigation service up to handle resolving the ViewModels from the IoC container, automatically supplying their dependencies through constructor injection, as shown in the following steps:

1. First, remove the code from the constructor of each Page that sets its `BindingContext` property to a new ViewModel instance.

2. Next, update the `NavigateToView` private method in the `XamarinFormsNavService` to handle setting the ViewModels of the Pages automatically as they are navigated to. After the Page (View) is created using the `Invoke` method, simply get a new instance of the specified ViewModel and assign it to the `BindingContext` property of the Page:

```
async Task NavigateToView(Type viewModelType)
{
    // ...

    var view = constructor.Invoke(null) as Page;

    var vm = ((App)Application.Current)
        .Kernel
        .GetService(viewModelType);

    view.BindingContext = vm;

    await XamarinFormsNav.PushAsync(view, true);
}
```

Summary

In this chapter, we explored the benefits of IoC and the dependency injection pattern in mobile development, and how they help solve the problem of working with platform-specific APIs from shared code. We also made some significant improvements to our Xamarin.Forms TripLog app by adding a new platform-specific service and introducing the Ninject dependency injection library, resulting in a code base that is more flexible and easier to test.

In the next chapter, we will shift our focus back to the View layer of our app and enhance the user experience with some customizations, and leverage some of the platform capabilities we are now showcasing through our ViewModels.

5
User Interface

In this chapter, we'll cover the following topics:

- Leveraging platform-specific APIs to extend the default behavior of Xamarin.Forms controls with **custom renderers**
- Manipulating the visual appearance of bound data with **value converters**
- Leveraging basic accessibility APIs so that a user interface is friendly and easy to use for all audiences

Custom renderers

One of the paramount features of the Xamarin.Forms toolkit is the layer of abstraction it provides over user interface implementation. With a single API, Xamarin.Forms allows you to use native user interface controls and functionality. For example, the `Entry` class at runtime will display a `UITextField` view on iOS, an `EditText` widget on Android, and a `TextBox` control on Windows. The toolkit does this using a concept called renderers. The renderers correspond with the visual elements—controls, pages, and layouts—within the API. So, for example, there is an `EntryRenderer` that is responsible for rendering instances of the `Entry` class down to the platform-specific versions of that control. The beauty of this renderer concept is that you can subclass the various renderer classes to override how a specific element is translated at runtime. So, for example, if you want all text boxes in your app (that is, every time you display an `Entry` element) to be completely borderless, you could simply write a new `EntryRenderer` subclass for each platform that removes the border on the platform-specific element.

However, you typically won't want to completely override the default controls of the toolkit. The most common solution is to create a custom control by subclassing a Xamarin.Forms element and then writing the renderer specifically for that custom class. So, instead of removing the border from all uses of Entry, you would instead use a custom Entry class, for example, NoBorderEntry, that, when rendered, will be borderless.

The concept of custom renderers is a very powerful and handy utility when building rich apps using the Xamarin.Forms toolkit. Using the default controls and behaviors of the toolkit will certainly render a native experience, but they can limit you in more complex scenarios. Custom renderers will ensure that you can exceed these limits when needed, to deliver the exact experience you want.

Creating a TableView DatePicker

In our TripLog app, we are using a TableView with EntryCell elements to present a form so the user can add a new log entry. Currently, the date field in the form uses a regular EntryCell that presents an editable text field with the default keyboard. Obviously, this is not an ideal user experience, and is also a nightmare when it comes to data validation. Ideally, when the user taps into this date field, they should be presented with a standard, platform-specific date picker.

The Xamarin.Forms API provides the DatePicker control; however, it is based on a View, not a ViewCell. The only way to use the DatePicker control in a TableView would be to wrap it in a ViewCell, as follows:

```
var datePickerCell = new ViewCell
{
    View = new DatePicker()
};
```

Or, in XAML, as follows:

```
<ViewCell>
    <DatePicker />
</ViewCell>
```

Although this approach will work, it is somewhat limited. It is simply a control embedded in a `ViewCell`; it does not have the same look and feel as the rest of the cells in the `TableView`. In order to get a similar look and feel to the other `EntryCell` elements used in the `TableView`, you will have to add a label and also mess with the margins, spacing, and sizing to get it to look just right. Another minor downside to this approach is that you will need to include two separate cells—one that includes `DatePicker` and one that includes `TimePicker`—in order to capture both date and time. The iOS `UIDatePicker` actually provides a mode that lets the user pick both the date and time in the same picker. Android does not have this same capability; however, if we're going to make a custom renderer, we can at least take advantage of the dual mode on iOS.

So, in order to overcome these limitations and deliver the best experience possible, we can create a custom renderer that extends the `EntryCellRenderer` to display an `EntryCell` that behaves like the standard `DatePicker` control.

Since we don't want to render all `EntryCell` elements in our application with the date picker functionality, the first thing that we will need to do is to create a custom `EntryCell` control that the custom renderer will be affiliated with. We can create this in a `Controls` folder within the core library of our TripLog app, as follows:

1. First, create a new folder in the core project named `Controls`.
2. Create a new class in the `Controls` folder named `DatePickerEntryCell` that inherits from `EntryCell`:

```
public class DatePickerEntryCell : EntryCell
{
}
```

3. Next, add a `DateTime BindableProperty` so that this custom control can be data bound just like any other control:

```
public class DatePickerEntryCell : EntryCell
{
    public static readonly BindableProperty DateProperty =
        BindableProperty.Create(
            nameof(Date),
            typeof(DateTime),
            typeof(DatePickerEntryCell),
            DateTime.Now,
            BindingMode.TwoWay);

    public DateTime Date
    {
```

```
        get { return (DateTime)GetValue(DateProperty); }
        set { SetValue(DateProperty, value); }
    }

    public new event EventHandler Completed;

    public void SendCompleted()
    {
        Completed?.Invoke(this, EventArgs.Empty);
    }
}
```

Notice how the `Completed EventHandler` is used in conjunction with the `DateProperty` `PropertyChanged` event so that we can respond to the `Completed` events on our `DatePickerEntryCell` just as we can with a standard `EntryCell`.

Next, we will need to create a custom `EntryCellRenderer`, which will provide the platform-specific functionality for the `DatePickerEntryCell`, as follows:

1. Create a new folder in the TripLog.iOS project named `Renderers`
2. Create a new class in the `Renderers` folder named `DatePickerEntryCellRenderer` that inherits from `EntryCellRenderer`, as follows:

```
public class DatePickerEntryCellRenderer : EntryCellRenderer
{
}
```

3. Next, override the `EntryCellRenderer GetCell` method to override the default `EntryCell` behavior for iOS by setting `InputView` of the `UITextField` to a `UIDatePicker` instance:

```
public class DatePickerEntryCellRenderer : EntryCellRenderer
{
    public override UITableViewCell GetCell(Cell item,
        UITableViewCell reusableCell, UITableView tv)
    {
        var cell = base.GetCell(item, reusableCell, tv);
        var datepickerCell = (DatePickerEntryCell)item;
        UITextField textField = null;

        if (cell != null)
        {
            textField = (UITextField)cell.ContentView.Subviews[0];
        }
```

```
// Default datepicker display attributes
var mode = UIDatePickerMode.Date;
var displayFormat = "d";
var date = NSDate.Now;
var isLocalTime = false;

// Update datepicker based on Cell's properties
if (datepickerCell != null)
{
    // Kind must be Universal or Local to cast to NSDate
    if (datepickerCell.Date.Kind == DateTimeKind.Unspecified)
    {
        var local = new DateTime(datepickerCell.Date.Ticks,
            DateTimeKind.Local);

        date = (NSDate)local;
    }
    else
    {
        date = (NSDate)datepickerCell.Date;
    }

    isLocalTime =
        datepickerCell.Date.Kind == DateTimeKind.Local
        || datepickerCell.Date.Kind ==
DateTimeKind.Unspecified;
}

// Create iOS datepicker
var datepicker = new UIDatePicker
{
    Mode = mode,
    BackgroundColor = UIColor.White,
    Date = date,
    TimeZone = isLocalTime
        ? NSTimeZone.LocalTimeZone
        : new NSTimeZone("UTC")
};

// Create a toolbar with a done button that will
// close the datepicker and set the selected value
var done = new UIBarButtonItem("Done",
    UIBarButtonItemStyle.Done, (s, e) =>
{
    var pickedDate = (DateTime)datepicker.Date;

    if (isLocalTime)
    {
```

```
                        pickedDate = pickedDate.ToLocalTime();
                    }

                    // Update the value of the UITextField within the Cell
                    if (textField != null)
                    {
                        textField.Text = pickedDate.ToString(displayFormat);
                        textField.ResignFirstResponder();
                    }

                    // Update the Date property on the Cell
                    if (datepickerCell != null)
                    {
                        datepickerCell.Date = pickedDate;
                        datepickerCell.SendCompleted();
                    }
                });

                var toolbar = new UIToolbar
                {
                    BarStyle = UIBarStyle.Default,
                    Translucent = false
                };

                toolbar.SizeToFit();
                toolbar.SetItems(new[] { done }, true);

                // Set the input view, toolbar and
                // initial value for the Cell's UITextField
                if (textField != null)
                {
                    textField.InputView = datepicker;
                    textField.InputAccessoryView = toolbar;

                    if (datepickerCell != null)
                    {
                        textField.Text = datepickerCell
                                        .Date.ToString(displayFormat);
                    }
                }

                return cell;
            }
        }
```

4. Next, in order to register the custom renderer, simply add an `ExportRenderer` assembly attribute to the class above the namespace declaration. This attribute is required by Xamarin.Forms in order for the custom renderer to take action on the control at runtime:

```
[assembly: ExportRenderer(typeof(DatePickerEntryCell),
                          typeof(DatePickerEntryCellRenderer))]
namespace TripLog.iOS.Renderers
{
    // ...
}
```

5. Finally, we will need to update the new entry XAML page to use our new custom `DatePickerEntryCell`. Simply update the date `EntryCell` tag, to a `DatePickerEntryCell` tag and the binding to use `DateProperty`. Also, ensure that you include the `Controls` namespace in the root `ContentPage` tag, as follows:

```
<ContentPage xmlns="http://xamarin.com/schemas/2014/forms"
    xmlns:x="http://schemas.microsoft.com/winfx/2009/xaml"
    xmlns:controls="clr-namespace:TripLog.Controls;assembly=TripLog"
    x:Class="TripLog.NewEntryPage"
    Title="New Entry">
    <ContentPage.Content>
        <TableView Intent="Form">
            <TableView.Root>
                <TableSection>
                    <EntryCell Label="Title" ... />
                    <EntryCell Label="Latitude" ... />
                    <EntryCell Label="Longitude" ... />
                    <controls:DatePickerEntryCell Label="Date"
                        Date="{Binding Date, StringFormat='{0:d}'}"/>
                    <EntryCell Label="Rating" ... />
                    <EntryCell Label="Notes" ... />
                </TableSection>
            </TableView.Root>
        </TableView>
    </ContentPage.Content>
</ContentPage>
```

Now, if we run the TripLog app, navigate to the new entry page, and tap into the date field, we will see a native date picker, as shown in the following screenshot. As we pick different values in the picker, the `DateProperty` binding we created will automatically update the ViewModel as well.

The Android version of this custom renderer is available in the companion source code for this book.

Value converters

Value converters form an important concept in data binding because they allow you to customize the appearance of a data property at the time of binding. If you have done any WPF or Windows app development, you will probably be familiar with how value converters work. Xamarin.Forms provides an almost identical value converter interface as part of its API.

One of the biggest benefits of a value converter is that it prevents you from having to add a bunch of getter properties to your data model to adjust how things are displayed. For example, imagine you have a status property on your model, and you want to change the font color of the status when it is displayed based on its value. You could add a `getter` property to your model that returns a color based on the current value of the status property. This approach works, but it clutters the model and also potentially leaks platform-specific and user interface logic into the model, which should typically remain very lean and agnostic. The more appropriate approach is to create a value converter that allows you to bind an element directly to the status property but display it differently based on the value.

Another common way that value converters are helpful in Xamarin.Forms is to toggle the visibility of elements based on a boolean property. Luckily, the Xamarin.Forms API made the `VisualElement IsVisible` property a boolean instead of an enumeration, so showing things based on boolean properties is fairly straightforward. However, if you want to hide something when a data bound property is true, you will need a value converter to convert the `true` value to a `false` value when it is bound to `IsVisibleProperty` of an element.

In the next section, we will create a reverse visibility converter which we will use to hide controls on the screen until the ViewModel has finished loading. We'll also create a converter that converts our integer rating property to stars, for a more appealing visual effect.

Creating a reverse visibility value converter

There are often cases where your user interface must wait for data to be loaded. In the meantime, the user might see what appears to be a broken or incomplete page. In these situations, it is best to let the user know what is happening by showing some sort of progress indicator and hiding the rest of the user interface, such as labels, until the data is ready.

Right now, our TripLog app uses only local data, so we do not really see any negative visual effects while the ViewModel data is loading. We will connect our app to a live API in the next chapter but, until then, we can simulate a waiting period by simply adding a three-second delay to our `NewEntryViewModel ExecuteSaveCommand()` method before the `NavService.GoBack()` method is called:

```
async Task ExecuteSaveCommand()
{
    // ...

    // TODO: Remove this in Chapter 6
    await Task.Delay(3000);

    await NavService.GoBack();
}
```

Now, when we run the app and add a new trip, we will see the UI freeze up for a few seconds before navigating back to the main page. Not only is this experience unappealing, but there is also no visual indicator to explain to the user that their data is being saved.

We can improve this by displaying an `ActivityIndicator` control while the new trip is being saved.

In order to know whether our ViewModel is saving (or loading) data, we can create a boolean property called `IsBusy`, which we will set to true only while we are actually loading data or doing some sort of lengthy processing, such as saving data. Since we will need to do similar things in other ViewModels, it makes the most sense to include this boolean `IsBusy` property in the `BaseViewModel`:

1. Add a public `bool` property named `IsBusy` to the `BaseViewModel` class, as follows:

   ```
   public abstract class BaseViewModel : INotifyPropertyChanged
   {
       // ...
   ```

```
bool _isBusy;
public bool IsBusy
{
    get { return _isBusy; }
    set
    {
        _isBusy = value;
        OnPropertyChanged();
        OnIsBusyChanged();
    }
}

protected virtual void OnIsBusyChanged()
{
}

// ...
}
```

2. Next, we will need to update the ExecuteSaveCommand() method in NewEntryViewModel to toggle the IsBusy value while it's saving data:

```
async Task ExecuteSaveCommand()
{
    if (IsBusy)
        return;

    IsBusy = true;

    try
    {
        // ...
    }
    finally
    {
        IsBusy = false;
    }
}
```

Now that our ViewModel indicates when it is busy, we will need to update the UI in NewEntryPage.xaml to hide the entry form while the trip is being saved, and show a spinner instead. We will do this by data binding the IsBusy property in two places. In order to hide the entry form TableView element when IsBusy is true, we will need to create a reverse boolean value converter.

1. Create a new folder in the core project named Converters.

2. Create new class file in the Converters folder named ReverseBooleanConverter that implements Xamarin.Forms.IValueConverter:

```
public class ReverseBooleanConverter : IValueConverter
{
}
```

3. Next, implement the Convert() and ConvertBack() methods of IValueConverter. The goal of this converter is to return the opposite of a given boolean value so, when something is false, the converter will return true:

```
public class ReverseBooleanConverter : IValueConverter
{
    public object Convert (object value,
        Type targetType, object parameter, CultureInfo culture)
    {
        if (!(value is Boolean))
        {
            return value;
        }

        return !((Boolean)value);
    }

    public object ConvertBack (object value,
        Type targetType, object parameter, CultureInfo culture)
    {
        if (!(value is Boolean))
        {
            return value;
        }

        return !((Boolean)value);
    }
}
```

4. Now we can bind the `IsBusy` property to the `TableView` element in `NewEntryPage.xaml` using this converter, so it is only visible (`IsVisible` is `true`) when `IsBusy` is `false`:

```
<ContentPage xmlns="http://xamarin.com/schemas/2014/forms"
    xmlns:x="http://schemas.microsoft.com/winfx/2009/xaml"
    xmlns:controls="clr-namespace:TripLog.Controls;assembly=TripLog"
    xmlns:converters="clr-
namespace:TripLog.Converters;assembly=TripLog"
    x:Class="TripLog.NewEntryPage"
    Title="New Entry">
    <ContentPage.Resources>
        <ResourceDictionary>
            <converters:ReverseBooleanConverter
                x:Key="ReverseBooleanConverter" />
        </ResourceDictionary>
    </ContentPage.Resources>
    <ContentPage.ToolbarItems>
        <ToolbarItem Text="Save" Command="{Binding SaveCommand}" />
    </ContentPage.ToolbarItems>
    <ContentPage.Content>
        <TableView Intent="Form"
            IsVisible="{Binding IsBusy, Converter={StaticResource
ReverseBooleanConverter}}">
            <TableView.Root>
                <TableSection>
                    <!-- ... -->
                </TableSection>
            </TableView.Root>
        </TableView>
    </ContentPage.Content>
</ContentPage>
```

Note that we must declare the `Converters` namespace in the root `ContentPage` tag and also define a static resource key for the converter so that it can be referenced within the binding.

5. Finally, we will need to add a loading indicator to `NewEntryPage.xaml` and only show it when `IsBusy` is true. We'll do this by adding an `ActivityIndicator` control and a `Label` control to a `StackLayout` view layout and displaying it in the center of the screen. Also, because we now have two elements to show on the screen, we will need to update how we're setting `Content` of `ContentPage` using a `Grid`:

```
<ContentPage.Content>
    <Grid>
        <TableView Intent="Form"
            IsVisible="{Binding IsBusy, Converter={StaticResource
ReverseBooleanConverter}}">

            <!-- ... -->

        </TableView>

        <StackLayout Orientation="Vertical"
            VerticalOptions="Center"
            HorizontalOptions="Center"
            IsVisible="{Binding IsBusy}">
            <ActivityIndicator IsRunning="True" />
            <Label Text="Saving new entry..." />
        </StackLayout>

    </Grid>
</ContentPage.Content>
```

Now, when we launch the app and save a new trip, we will see a nice loading indicator while the data saves instead of a frozen UI, as shown in the following screenshot:

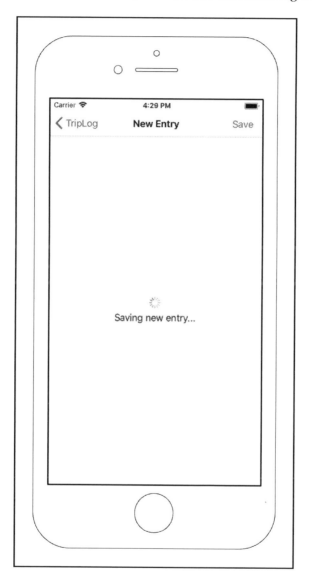

Creating an integer to image value converter

In this section, we will continue to improve the user experience with the use of another value converter. Currently, the detail page binds to the Rating property and simply displays the integer value as a formatted string, which is a rather boring way to display data, as shown in the following screenshot:

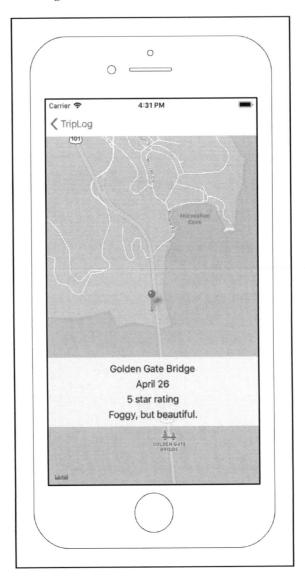

This rating data would look much nicer, and stand out to the user much more if it were an image of stars instead of plain text. In order to translate a number value to an image, we will need to create a new value converter, as shown in the following steps:

1. Create a new class file in the core library `Converters` folder named `RatingToStarImageNameConverter` that implements `Xamarin.Forms.IValueConverter`:

```
public class RatingToStarImageNameConverter : IValueConverter
{
}
```

2. Next, provide implementations for the `Convert` and `ConvertBack` methods of `IValueConverter`. In the `Convert` method, we will need to check whether the value is an integer, and then, based on its value, we will need to convert it to an image filename:

```
public class RatingToStarImageNameConverter : IValueConverter
{
    public object Convert(object value,
        Type targetType, object parameter, CultureInfo culture)
    {
        if (value is int)
        {
            var rating = (int)value;

            if (rating <= 1)
            {
                return "star_1";
            }

            if (rating >= 5)
            {
                return "stars_5";
            }

            return "stars_" + rating;
        }

        return value;
    }

    public object ConvertBack(object value,
        Type targetType, object parameter, CultureInfo culture)
    {
        throw new NotImplementedException();
```

```
        }
    }
```

3. Finally, we will need to update `DetailPage.xaml` to use an `Image` control instead of a `Label` to display the rating. We will still bind the `Image` control to the same ViewModel property; however, we will use the converter we just created to convert it to an image filename:

```
<ContentPage xmlns="http://xamarin.com/schemas/2014/forms"
    xmlns:x="http://schemas.microsoft.com/winfx/2009/xaml"
    xmlns:maps="clr-
namespace:Xamarin.Forms.Maps;assembly=Xamarin.Forms.Maps"
    xmlns:converters="clr-
namespace:TripLog.Converters;assembly=TripLog"
    x:Class="TripLog.DetailPage">
    <ContentPage.Resources>
        <ResourceDictionary>
            <converters:RatingToStarImageNameConverter
                x:Key="RatingToStartImageNameConverter" />
        </ResourceDictionary>
    </ContentPage.Resources>
    <ContentPage.Content>
        <Grid>

            <!-- ... -->

            <StackLayout Padding="10" Grid.Row="1">
                <Label HorizontalOptions="Center"
                    Text="{Binding Entry.Title}" />
                <Label HorizontalOptions="Center"
                    Text="{Binding Entry.Date,
                                StringFormat='{0:M}'}" />
                <Image HorizontalOptions="Center"
                    Source="{Binding Entry.Rating,
Converter={StaticResource RatingToStartImageNameConverter}}" />
                <Label HorizontalOptions="Center"
                    Text="{Binding Entry.Notes}" />
            </StackLayout>
        </Grid>
    </ContentPage.Content>
</ContentPage>
```

Now, if we run the app and navigate to one of the entries, we will see a much nicer display that immediately causes the rating to stand out to the user, as shown in the following screenshot:

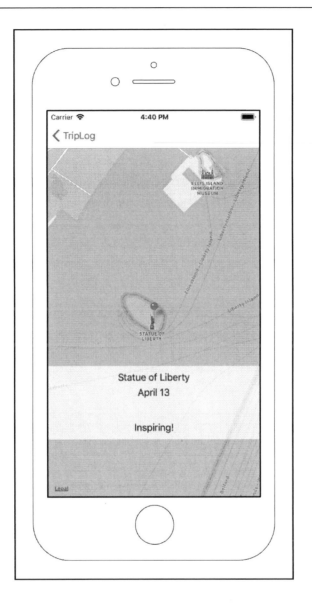

 The images used for the star rating are available in the companion code for this book.

Adding pull-to-refresh

As with the new entry page, when the main page is loading our data, we should present the user with a loading indicator so that they know their list of entries is on its way. However, since the main page is using a data-bound `ListView` instead of a static `TableView`, we can use the `ListView` pull-to-refresh functionality to indicate when our data is being loaded. Pull-to-refresh also has the benefit of allowing users to easily refresh the screen and load any new data that might be available. Xamarin.Forms makes adding pull-to-refresh very easy, and we will still use the `IsBusy` property from our `BaseViewModel`, just as we did on the new entry page.

The Xamarin.Forms `ListView` pull-to-refresh API requires two things: an `ICommand` that handles refreshing the bound source of the `ListView`, and a boolean field that indicates whether the `ListView` is currently refreshing or not. To add pull-to-refresh, perform the following steps:

1. First, we will need to add a new refresh command to `MainViewModel`. This command will simply call the existing `LoadEntries()` method:

```
Command _refreshCommand;
public Command RefreshCommand
{
    get
    {
        return _refreshCommand
            ?? (_refreshCommand = new Command(
                async () => await LoadEntries()));
    }
}
```

2. Next, we will need to update the `LoadEntries` method to set `IsBusy` while it's loading its data. For now, just as we did earlier in the chapter with the `NewEntryViewModel`, we will add a three-second delay to simulate a waiting period (we will remove this in the next chapter when we start getting our data from a live web service):

```
async Task LoadEntries()
{
    if (IsBusy)
    {
        return;
    }

    IsBusy = true;
```

```
LogEntries.Clear();

// TODO: Remove this in chapter 6
await Task.Delay(3000);

LogEntries.Add(new TripLogEntry
{
    // ...
});

LogEntries.Add(new TripLogEntry
{
    // ...
});

LogEntries.Add(new TripLogEntry
{
    // ...
});

IsBusy = false;
}
```

3. Next, we will need to update the `ListView` tag in `MainPage.xaml` to enable pull-to-refresh and to bind its `RefreshCommand` property to the new `RefreshCommand` command we just added in `MainViewModel`. For the `ListView` `IsRefreshing` property, we can simply bind to `IsBusy`, as that will be set to true while we're loading entries and back to false when that operation is complete:

```
<ListView ... ItemsSource="{Binding LogEntries"
    IsPullToRefreshEnabled="True"
    IsRefreshing="{Binding IsBusy, Mode=OneWay}"
    RefreshCommand="{Binding RefreshCommand}">
```

Now when we run the app, we will see the pull-to-refresh spinner while the data initially loads on the main page, as well as when the user pulls down on the list, as shown in the following screenshot:

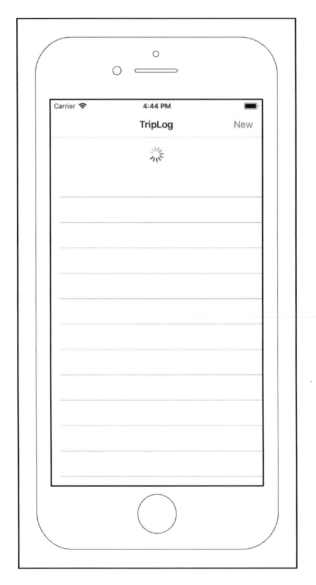

Accessibility

When it comes to user interfaces, accessibility is often an afterthought or forgotten about completely. User interfaces are not just about good-looking icons, fonts, and fancy custom controls, they are also about how your users actually use the app. This means that you need to leverage the platform's accessibility APIs to ensure usability for as much of your potential audience as possible. Xamarin.Forms now provides some basic APIs for adding accessibility to your apps, so users who depend on screen readers can successfully interact with the screens of your app.

Supporting screen readers

One of the most common ways to bring accessibility to an app is to provide support for screen readers, which are used to narrate and describe elements on the screen. In this section, we will use the Xamarin.Forms `AutomationProperties` class to easily add screen reader support to our entry detail page:

1. First, we will need to update each of the detail elements in `DetailPage.xaml` to be included in the accessibility tree, making them readable by the operating systems' screen readers:

```
<StackLayout Padding="10" Grid.Row="1">
    <Label ... Text="{Binding Entry.Title}"
        AutomationProperties.IsInAccessibleTree="true" />
    <Label ... Text="{Binding Entry.Date, StringFormat='{0:M}'}"
        AutomationProperties.IsInAccessibleTree="true" />
    <Image ... Source="{Binding Entry.Rating,
 Converter={StaticResource RatingToStartImageNameConverter}}"
        AutomationProperties.IsInAccessibleTree="true" />
    <Label ... Text="{Binding Entry.Notes}"
        AutomationProperties.IsInAccessibleTree="true" />
</StackLayout>
```

2. Next, we will need to update each of the detail elements in `DetailPage.xaml` to describe itself. This is what the screen reader will use when narrating. There are a couple of properties that we can use for this, such as `AutomationProperties.Name` and `AutomationProperties.HelpText`. `Name` is used to identify the element, while `HelpText` is used to describe what the element is used for or what type of data should be provided to the element, as shown in the following code:

```
<StackLayout Padding="10" Grid.Row="1">
    <Label ... Text="{Binding Entry.Title}"
        AutomationProperties.IsInAccessibleTree="true"
        AutomationProperties.HelpText="Title of trip" />
    <Label ... Text="{Binding Entry.Date, StringFormat='{0:M}'}"
        AutomationProperties.IsInAccessibleTree="true"
        AutomationProperties.HelpText="Date of trip" />
    <Image ... Source="{Binding Entry.Rating,
Converter={StaticResource RatingToStartImageNameConverter}}"
        AutomationProperties.IsInAccessibleTree="true"
        AutomationProperties.HelpText="{Binding Entry.Rating,
StringFormat='{0} star rating'}" />
    <Label ... Text="{Binding Entry.Notes}"
        AutomationProperties.IsInAccessibleTree="true"
        AutomationProperties.HelpText="Notes from trip" />
</StackLayout>
```

Notice how we used data binding to set the `AutomationProperties.HelpText` attribute for the rating `Image` tag.

Each platform handles accessibility and screen reading differently—using different combinations and precedence of the `AutomationProperties` attached properties. Refer to the Xamarin.Forms accessibility documentation and the accessibility documentation specific to each platform for more details.

Summary

In this chapter, we leveraged several key concepts in the Xamarin.Forms API to help improve the look, feel, and user experience of our TripLog app. With the use of a custom renderer, we are now able to tap directly into the platform-specific APIs to change the default behavior of Xamarin.Forms controls and, with the use of value converters, we are now able to alter the appearance of data when it is bound to the user interface. Finally, the Xamarin.Forms accessibility APIs give us the ability to make our app more straightforward for users who rely on accessibility features to use their mobile apps.

In the next chapter, we will connect the TripLog app to an API in order to work with live data.

6
API Data Access

So far in this book, we have worked with static data that is hardcoded directly into the TripLog app itself. However, in the real world, it is rare that an app depends purely on local static data—most mobile apps get their data from a remote data source, typically an API. In some cases, an app may communicate with a third-party API, that of a social network, for example. Alternatively, developers sometimes create their own API to make data available for their apps. In this chapter, we will create a simple API in the cloud that we can connect to and retrieve data from in the TripLog app.

The following is a quick look at what we will cover in this chapter:

- Creating a live, cloud-based, backend service and API using Microsoft's Azure App Service platform to store and retrieve TripLog data
- Creating a data access service that handles communication with the API for the TripLog mobile app
- Setting up data caching so that the TripLog app works offline

Creating an API with Microsoft's Azure App Service

Almost all mobile apps communicate with an API to retrieve and store information. In many cases, as a mobile app developer, you might just have to use an API that already exists. However, if you're building your own product or service, you may need to create your own backend and web API. There are several ways you can create an API, several places you can host it, and certainly many different languages you can develop it in. For the purposes of this book, we will create a backend service and web API in the cloud using Microsoft's Azure App Services. Azure App Services contains many products and features, one of which is called Mobile Apps (formally known as Azure Mobile Services).

Azure Mobile Apps provide a very quick and easy way to get a fully functional backend service up and running in a matter of minutes. You can create the backend service using either Node.js or .NET. Since the primary focus of this book is developing a mobile app, I will not spend a lot of time explaining every small detail of the Azure Mobile Apps product. So, in this section, we will just cover the basics needed to create a simple API that we can connect our app to later in this chapter.

In order to follow along with the steps in this chapter, you will need to have an Azure account. If you don't already have an Azure account, you can create one for free at `https://azure.microsoft.com/en-us/pricing/free-trial/`.

Once you have an Azure account, you can then begin setting up a mobile backend and API in the Azure portal, as follows:

1. Go to `https://portal.azure.com` in a web browser, and log in to the Azure portal using your credentials.

2. From the main Azure portal dashboard, click on the **+ New** button in the top-left-hand corner, then click on the **Web + Mobile** option and select **Mobile App**, as shown in the following screenshot:

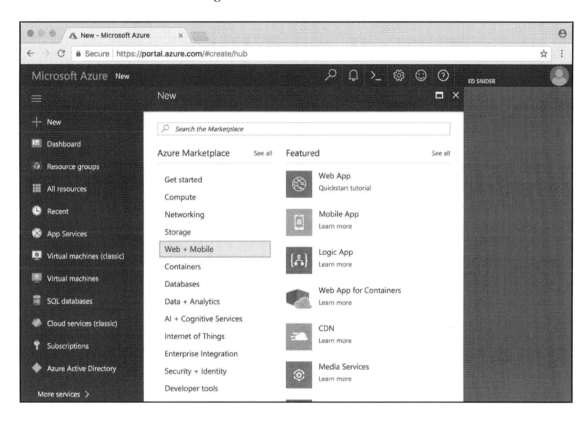

3. Enter a name for your service in the far-right **Mobile App** pane:

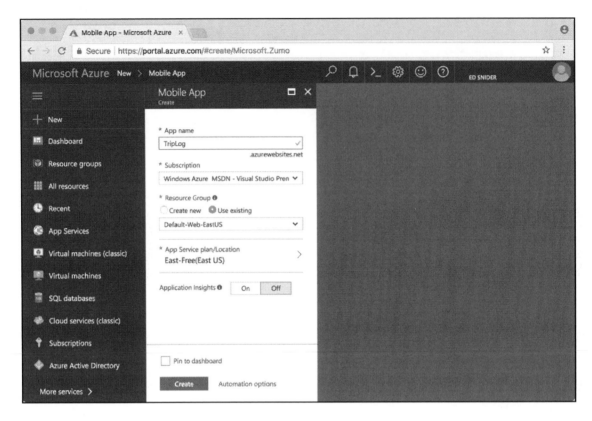

4. Select your **Subscription, Resource Group**, and **App Service Plan/Location** by taking the defaults or creating new ones.

5. Click the **Create** button.

6. Once your new service has been created, navigate to it from the dashboard.

7. Next, we will need to set up the database that will store the data for the App Service. Select **Data Connections** from the **MOBILE** section of the **Mobile App** settings pane to set up a new data connection, as shown in the following screenshot:

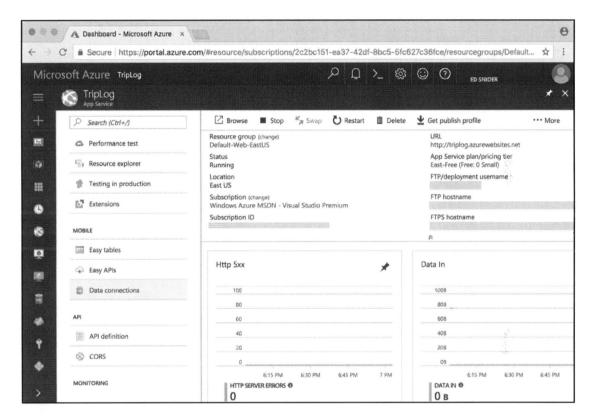

Once you have created a new Mobile App in Azure, it will, by default, have no tables or data. Before we can start working with the API, we will need to create a table to store our data by following these steps:

1. Select **Easy tables** from the **MOBILE** section of the Mobile App settings pane.
2. Click on the **Add** button. If this is the first table in the service, you may be prompted to configure the service to use **Easy Tables** before creating a new table.

When you configure an app service to use Easy Tables from within the
Azure portal, it will automatically create a Node.js backend for the service.
If you want to use a .NET backend instead, take a look at the
documentation at `https://docs.microsoft.com/en-us/azure/app-`
`service-mobile/app-service-mobile-dotnet-backend-how-to-use-`
`server-sdk`.

3. Name the new table **Entry**, and ensure that all the permissions are set to **Allow
    anonymous access**, as shown in the following screenshot:

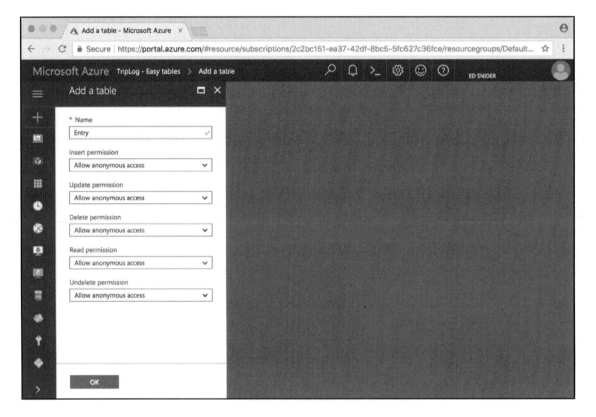

4. Click on **OK** and the new table will be added to the list of **Easy Tables**.

By selecting the **Allow anonymous access** permission, we are making the API available
without providing any specific authentication headers in the HTTP request. In the next
chapter, we will add authentication to both the API and the mobile app, but for now we will
simply provide anonymous access.

Browsing and adding data

Now that we have created an API in Azure and set up a data table within the service, we can start making calls to the API and getting responses. Before we start making calls to the API from within the TripLog app, we can test the endpoint by making GET and POST HTTP requests to it using either a command line or a REST console.

There are several REST consoles to choose from if you don't already have one installed. I typically use a Google Chrome plugin named **JaSON** (`https://github.com/shanebell/JaSON`) or an app named **Postman** (`http://www.getpostman.com`).

 If you don't want to use a REST console, you can use the command line to issue HTTP requests to the API. To do this, use either `curl` in the Terminal on macOS or `Invoke-RestMethod` in PowerShell on Windows.

1. Using either a REST console or the command line, issue a GET request to the API endpoint for the Entry table using the following URL and header:

   ```
   https://<your-service-name>.azurewebsites.net/tables/entry
   --header "zumo-api-version:2.0.0"
   ```

2. If everything has been set up properly, we should receive a 200 status code and an empty collection in the response body, as follows:

   ```
   []
   ```

3. Next, add a new record to the backend service by issuing a POST request to the same API endpoint, with an Entry JSON object included in the body of the request. The service will automatically create the appropriate columns within the Entry table when we insert the first object and we should get a 200 status code with the new item we added in the response body, as follows:

   ```
   https://<your-service-name>.azurewebsites.net/tables/entry
   --header "zumo-api-version:2.0.0"
   --header "Content-Type:application/json"
   --data '{
           "title": "Space Needle",
           "latitude": 47.6204,
           "longitude": -122.3491,
           "date": "2017-07-05T00:00:00.000Z",
           "rating": 5,
           "notes": "Wonderful site to see"
       }'
   ```

4. Next, issue another GET request to the entry endpoint:

```
https://<your-service-name>.azurewebsites.net/tables/entry
--header "zumo-api-version:2.0.0"
```

We should receive a 200 status code, but now the response body has a collection containing the new item we added:

```
[
    {
        "id": "c4a0595d-ac77-4c5b-9d94-f70374e522ab",
        "createdAt": "2017-07-05T21:37:41.946Z",
        "updatedAt": "2017-07-05T21:37:41.946Z",
        "version": "AAAAAAAAAAA=",
        "deleted": false,
        "title": "Space Needle",
        "latitude": 47.6204,
        "longitude": -122.3491,
        "date": "2017-07-05T00:00:00.000Z",
        "rating": 5,
        "notes": "Wonderful site to see"
    }
]
```

In the preceding response, notice that after we added the new record to the backend service, it was automatically given an id property, along with a couple of other properties. The id property serves as a unique primary key for the record. We will need to update the TripLogEntry model in our TripLog app to account for this new property, as shown in the following steps:

1. Add the **Json.NET** NuGet package to the core library project and each of the platform-specific projects.
2. Add a new string property named Id to the TripLogEntry model class, as follows:

```
public class TripLogEntry
{
    [JsonProperty("id")]
    public string Id { get; set; }
    public string Title { get; set; }
    public double Latitude { get; set; }
    public double Longitude { get; set; }
    public DateTime Date { get; set; }
    public int Rating { get; set; }
    public string Notes { get; set; }
}
```

Now that we have a live backend service that we can communicate with via HTTP, we will update our TripLog app so that it can send requests to the API to add and retrieve log entries.

Creating a base HTTP service

In order for an app to communicate with an API via HTTP, it needs an HTTP library. Since we are using .NET and C# to build a Xamarin.Forms app, we can leverage a library within the .NET Framework, called `System.Net.Http.HttpClient`. The .NET `HttpClient` provides a mechanism to send and receive data via standard HTTP methods, such as `GET` and `POST`.

Continuing to keep separation and abstraction key to our app architecture, we want to keep the specific logic related to the `HttpClient` separate from the rest of the app. In order to do this, we will write a base service class in our core library that will be responsible for handling HTTP communications in a generic way. This provides a building block for any domain-specific data services we might need to write, for example, a service that is responsible for working with log entries in the API. Any class that will inherit from this class will be able to send HTTP request messages using standard HTTP methods (such as `GET`, `POST`, `PATCH`, and `DELETE`) and get HTTP response messages back without having to deal with `HttpClient` directly.

As we saw in the previous section, we are able to post data to the API in the form of JSON, and when we receive data from the API, it's also returned in the JSON format. In order for our app to translate its C# models into JSON for use in an HTTP request body, the model will need to be serialized. In contrast, when an HTTP response message is received in JSON, it needs to be deserialized into the appropriate C# model. The most widely used method to do this in .NET software is to use the **Json.NET** library.

In order to create a base HTTP service, perform the following steps:

1. Add the **Microsoft.Net.Http** NuGet package to the core library project.
2. Create a new abstract class in the `Services` folder of the core library named `BaseHttpService`:

```
public abstract class BaseHttpService
{
}
```

3. Add a protected async method to the `BaseHttpService` class named `SendRequestAsync<T>` that takes in a `Uri` named `url`, an optional `HttpMethod` named `httpMethod`, an optional `IDictionary<string, string>` named `headers`, and an optional `object` named `requestData`. These four parameters will be used to construct an HTTP request. The `url` parameter is the full URL of the API endpoint for the request. The `httpMethod` optional parameter is used to make the request a `GET`, `POST`, and so on. The `headers` optional dictionary parameter is a collection of `string` key/value pairs used to define the header(s) of the request (such as authentication.) Finally, the `requestData` optional parameter is used to pass in an `object` that will be serialized into JSON and included in the body of `POST` and `PATCH` requests:

```
public abstract class BaseHttpService
{
    protected async Task<T> SendRequestAsync<T>(
        Uri url,
        HttpMethod httpMethod = null,
        IDictionary<string, string> headers = null,
        object requestData = null)
    {
        var result = default(T);

        // Default to GET
        var method = httpMethod ?? HttpMethod.Get;

        // Serialize request data
        var data = requestData == null
            ? null
            : JsonConvert.SerializeObject(requestData);

        using (var request = new HttpRequestMessage(method, url))
        {
            // Add request data to request
            if (data != null)
            {
                request.Content = new StringContent(
                    data, Encoding.UTF8, "application/json");
            }

            // Add headers to request
            if (headers != null)
            {
                foreach (var h in headers)
                {
                    request.Headers.Add(h.Key, h.Value);
```

```
            }
        }

        // Get response
        using (var handler = new HttpClientHandler())
        {
            using (var client = new HttpClient(handler))
            {
                using (var response = await client
                    .SendAsync(request, HttpCompletionOption
                        .ResponseContentRead))
                {
                    var content = response.Content == null
                        ? null
                        : await response.Content
                                        .ReadAsStringAsync();

                    if (response.IsSuccessStatusCode)
                    {
                        result = JsonConvert
                            .DeserializeObject<T>(content);
                    }
                }
            }
        }

        return result;
    }
}
```

Now that we have a base HTTP service, we can subclass it with classes that are more specific to our data model, which we will do in the next section.

Creating an API data service

Using `BaseHttpService` as a foundation that abstracts away the HTTP request details, we can now begin to create services that leverage it to get responses back from the API in the form of domain-specific models. Specifically, we will create a data service that can be used by the ViewModels to get the `TripLogEntry` objects from the backend service.

We will start off by defining an interface for the data service that can be injected into the ViewModels, ensuring that there is no strict dependency on the API, or the logic that communicates with it, continuing the pattern we put in place in Chapter 4, *Platform Specific Services and Dependency Injection*. To create a data service for the TripLog API, perform the following steps:

1. Create a new interface named ITripLogDataService in the Services folder of the core library:

```
public interface ITripLogDataService
{ }
```

2. Update the ITripLogDataService interface with methods to get, update, and delete TripLogEntry objects:

```
public interface ITripLogDataService
{
    Task<IList<TripLogEntry>> GetEntriesAsync();
    Task<TripLogEntry> GetEntryAsync(string id);
    Task<TripLogEntry> AddEntryAsync(TripLogEntry entry);
    Task<TripLogEntry> UpdateEntryAsync(TripLogEntry entry);
    Task RemoveEntryAsync(TripLogEntry entry);
}
```

Next, we will create an implementation of this interface that will also subclass BaseHttpService so that it has access to our HttpClient implementation, as shown in the following steps:

1. Create a new class in the core library Services folder named TripLogApiDataService that subclasses BaseHttpService and implements ITripLogDataService:

```
public class TripLogApiDataService
    : BaseHttpService, ITripLogDataService
{ }
```

2. Add two private properties to the `TripLogApiDataService` class—a `Uri` and an `IDictionary<string, string>`—to store the base URL and headers, respectively, to be used for all requests:

```
public class TripLogApiDataService
    : BaseHttpService, ITripLogDataService
{
    readonly Uri _baseUri;
    readonly IDictionary<string, string> _headers;
}
```

3. Update the `TripLogApiDataService` constructor to take in a `Uri` parameter, then set the private _baseUri and _headers properties:

```
public class TripLogApiDataService
    : BaseHttpService, ITripLogDataService
{
    readonly Uri _baseUri;
    readonly IDictionary<string, string> _headers;

    public TripLogApiDataService(Uri baseUri)
    {
        _baseUri = baseUri;
        _headers = new Dictionary<string, string>();

        // TODO: Add header with auth-based token in chapter 7
        _headers.Add ("zumo-api-version", "2.0.0");
    }
}
```

4. Finally, implement the members of `ITripLogDataService` using the `SendRequestAsync<T>` base class method:

```
public class TripLogApiDataService
    : BaseHttpService, ITripLogDataService
{
    readonly Uri _baseUri;
    readonly IDictionary<string, string> _headers;

    // ...

    public async Task<IList<TripLogEntry>> GetEntriesAsync()
    {
        var url = new Uri(_baseUri, "/tables/entry");
        var response = await SendRequestAsync<TripLogEntry[]>(url,
            HttpMethod.Get, _headers);
```

```
        return response;
    }

    public async Task<TripLogEntry> GetEntryAsync(string id)
    {
        var url = new Uri(_baseUri,
            string.Format("/tables/entry/{0}", id));
        var response = await SendRequestAsync<TripLogEntry>(url,
            HttpMethod.Get, _headers);

        return response;
    }

    public async Task<TripLogEntry> AddEntryAsync(TripLogEntry entry)
    {
        var url = new Uri(_baseUri, "/tables/entry");
        var response = await SendRequestAsync<TripLogEntry>(url,
            HttpMethod.Post, _headers, entry);

        return response;
    }

    public async Task<TripLogEntry> UpdateEntryAsync(TripLogEntry
entry)
    {
        var url = new Uri(_baseUri,
            string.Format("/tables/entry/{0}", entry.Id));
        var response = await SendRequestAsync<TripLogEntry>(url,
            new HttpMethod("PATCH"), _headers, entry);

        return response;
    }

    public async Task RemoveEntryAsync(TripLogEntry entry)
    {
        var url = new Uri(_baseUri,
            string.Format("/tables/entry/{0}", entry.Id));
        var response = await SendRequestAsync<TripLogEntry>(url,
            HttpMethod.Delete, _headers);
    }
}
```

Each method in this TripLog data service calls the `SendRequestAsync` method on the base class passing in the API route, the appropriate `HttpMethod`, and the `zumo-api-version` header that we used in the first section. The `AddEntryAsync` and `UpdateEntryAsync` methods also pass in a `TripLogEntry` object, which will be serialized and added to the HTTP request message content. In the next chapter, we will implement authentication with the API and update this service to pass in an authentication-based token in the header as well.

Updating the TripLog app ViewModels

Using the API and data service we created, we can now update the ViewModels in the app to use live data instead of the local, hardcoded data they currently use. We will continue to leverage the patterns we put in place in previous chapters to ensure that our ViewModels remain testable and do not have any specific dependencies on the Azure API, or even the HTTP communication logic. To update the ViewModels, perform the following steps:

1. First, update the `TripLogCoreModule` in the core library to register our `ITripLogDataService` implementation into the IoC:

```
public class TripLogCoreModule : NinjectModule
{
    public override void Load()
    {
        // ViewModels
        Bind<MainViewModel>().ToSelf();
        Bind<DetailViewModel>().ToSelf();
        Bind<NewEntryViewModel>().ToSelf();

        // Core Services
        var tripLogService = new TripLogApiDataService(new
            Uri("https://<your-service-name>.azurewebsites.net"));

        Bind<ITripLogDataService>()
            .ToMethod(x => tripLogService)
            .InSingletonScope();
    }
}
```

2. Next, update the `MainViewModel` constructor to take an `ITripLogDataService` parameter, which will be provided automatically via dependency injection:

```
readonly ITripLogDataService _tripLogService;

public MainViewModel(INavService navService,
    ITripLogDataService tripLogService)
    : base(navService)
{
    _tripLogService = tripLogService;

    LogEntries = new ObservableCollection<TripLogEntry>();
}
```

3. We will then update the `LoadEntries` method in `MainViewModel`, replacing the three-second delay and hardcoded data population with a call to the live TripLog API via the current `ITripLogDataService` implementation that is injected into the ViewModel's constructor:

```
async Task LoadEntries()
{
    if (IsBusy)
        return;

    IsBusy = true;

    try
    {
        var entries = await _tripLogService.GetEntriesAsync();

        LogEntries = new ObservableCollection<TripLogEntry>(entries);
    }
    finally
    {
        IsBusy = false;
    }
}
```

No other changes to `MainViewModel` are required. Now, when the app is launched, instead of the hardcoded data loading, you will see the items stored in the Azure backend service database.

Now, we will update the `NewEntryViewModel` so that when we add a new entry, it is actually saved to the Azure backend through the data service:

1. Update the `NewEntryViewModel` constructor to take an `ITripLogDataService` parameter:

```
readonly ITripLogDataService _tripLogService;

public NewEntryViewModel(INavService navService,
                         ILocationService locService,
                         ITripLogDataService tripLogService)
    : base(navService)
{
    _locService = locService;
    _tripLogService = tripLogService;

    Date = DateTime.Today;
    Rating = 1;
}
```

2. Then, we will update the `SaveCommand` execution method to call the `AddEntryAsync` method of the data service:

```
async Task ExecuteSaveCommand()
{
    if (IsBusy)
        return;

    IsBusy = true;

    try
    {
        var newItem = new TripLogEntry
        {
            Title = this.Title,
            Latitude = this.Latitude,
            Longitude = this.Longitude,
            Date = this.Date,
            Rating = this.Rating,
            Notes = this.Notes
        };

        await _tripLogService.AddEntryAsync(newItem);
        await NavService.GoBack();
    }
    finally
```

```
    {
        IsBusy = false;
    }
}
```

Now, if we launch the app, navigate to the new entry page, fill out the form, and click on **Save**, the log entry will be sent to the TripLog backend service and saved in the database.

Offline data caching

Mobile apps have several benefits over web apps, one of which is the ability to operate offline and maintain offline data. There are a couple of reasons why offline data is important to a mobile app. First of all, you cannot guarantee that your app will always have a network connection and the ability to directly connect to live data. Supporting offline data allows users to use the app, even if only for limited use cases when they are operating with limited or no connectivity. Secondly, users expect mobile apps to offer high performance, specifically, quick access to data without having to wait. By maintaining an offline cache, an app can present a user with data immediately while it's busy retrieving a fresh dataset, providing a perceived level of performance to the user. It is important that when the cache updates, the user receives that updated data automatically so that they are always seeing the latest data possible, depending on specific use cases of course.

There are several ways of implementing a data cache in a mobile app, all depending on the size and complexity of the data that needs to be stored. In most cases, storing the cache in a local database using SQLite is the best approach.

In this chapter, we will update the TripLog app to maintain a cache of log entries and keep the cache in sync with the live API as data is received from Azure backend service. The data cache will be stored in a SQLite database, but to ease the implementation, we will use an open source library called **Akavache**. Akavache provides not only caching capabilities, but also a very easy-to-use API to update the cache to be able to handle many different scenarios.

 For the purposes of this book and the TripLog sample application, we will only be using a small subset of the Akavache features. For a closer look at the Akavache library and all of its capabilities, check it out on GitHub at `https://github.com/akavache/Akavache`.

Adding the Akavache library

Like most libraries that we have used throughout this book, the Akavache library can be obtained via NuGet. First, add a reference to the library, including all of its dependencies, to the core library project and each of the platform-specific projects.

Next, we will need to add Akavache to our IoC container so that it can be injected into our ViewModels. Akavache comes with some static variables that make it very easy to use. However, we want to instead instantiate our own instance and add it to the IoC to maintain separation. To do this, update the `Load` method in the `TripLogCoreModule` Ninject module, as follows:

```
Bind<Akavache.IBlobCache>().ToConstant(Akavache.BlobCache.LocalMachine);
```

Maintaining an offline data cache

Currently, the TripLog app's `MainViewModel` calls the `TripLogApiDataService` to get its data directly from the live API. As mentioned at the beginning of this chapter, in the event of little or no connectivity, the TripLog app will fail to display any log entries. With a few minor modifications to the `MainViewModel`, we can set it up to use the Akavache library to retrieve log entries from a local cache, and also to refresh that cache with any changes in the dataset once a connection with a live API succeeds.

First, update the `MainViewModel` constructor to require an instance of `Akavache.IBlobCache`, which will be injected via our Ninject implementation from `Chapter 4`, *Platform-Specific Services and Dependency Injection*:

```
readonly IBlobCache _cache;

// ...

public MainViewModel(INavService navService,
                     ITripLogDataService tripLogService,
                     IBlobCache cache)
    : base (navService)
{
    _tripLogService = tripLogService;
    _cache = cache;

    LogEntries = new ObservableCollection<TripLogEntry> ();
}
```

Next, we will need to modify the logic in the LoadEntries method to tie into the local offline cache. To do this, we will leverage an extension method in Akavache called GetAndFetchLatest. This method actually performs two functions. First, it immediately returns cached data, given a specific key (in our case, entries). Secondly, it makes a call to the API based on the given Func<> and updates the cache for the given key. Since it is performing two functions, it will ultimately return twice. In order to handle this, and because it is returning an IObservable, we can use the Subscribe extension method to handle each return as it occurs. In the Subscribe extension method, we will update the LogEntries ObservableCollection property on the MainViewModel based on what is either returned from the cache or from the subsequent API call, if successful:

```
public override async Task Init()
{
    LoadEntries();
}

void LoadEntries()
{
    if (IsBusy)
    {
        return;
    }

    IsBusy = true;

    try
    {
        // Load from local cache and then immediately load from API
        _cache.GetAndFetchLatest("entries", async ()
                => await _tripLogService.GetEntriesAsync())
            .Subscribe(entries
                => LogEntries = new
    ObservableCollection<TripLogEntry>(entries));
    }
    finally
    {
        IsBusy = false;
    }
}
```

In the preceding code, notice that, because we're calling GetAndFetchLatest and using the Subscribe method, the LoadEntries method is no longer async, so ensure that you update the RefreshCommand execution Action as well.

The first time the app is launched with this code, the cache will be populated. On any subsequent launches of the app, you will notice that data appears immediately as the view is constructed. If you add an item to the backend service database and then launch the app again, you will notice that the new item falls into place after a couple of seconds.

Summary

In this chapter, we created a live API from scratch using Azure App Services. We then created a data service within our app to handle communication between the app and the API. Then, by adding a reference to this service to our ViewModels, we quickly transformed the app from using static data to using live data from our new API. Finally, we setup offline data caching.

In the next chapter, we will add authentication to our API and update the app with sign-in capabilities.

7
Authentication

In this chapter, we'll cover the following topics:

- Adding authentication to the Azure Mobile App Service
- Using the Xamarin.Auth library to easily perform OAuth and securely communicate with the API
- Updating the TripLog app with a sign in page

Adding identity and authentication to Azure Mobile Apps

In the previous chapter, we set up a new, live backend using an Azure Mobile App Service. The service contains a single table named Entry, which houses all log entries for our TripLog app. Currently, the Entry table is available anonymously. In this section, we will change the permissions on the Entry table to require each request to contain an access token associated with an authenticated user.

Setting up permissions

In order to enforce authentication to access our backend service, we will need to make a simple configuration change to the `Entry` table:

1. Select your TripLog App Service in the Azure portal.
2. Click on **Easy Tables** in the **MOBILE** section in the left-side pane and then select the **Entry** table, as shown in the following screenshot:

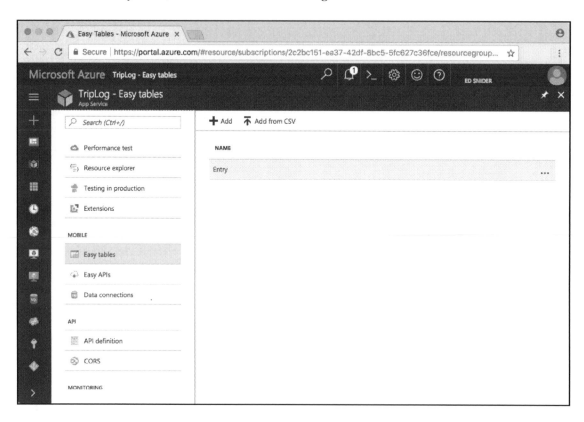

3. Click on **Change Permissions**.
4. Change each of the table permissions to **Authenticated access only**. Then, click on the **Save** button at the top of the pane, as shown in the following screenshot:

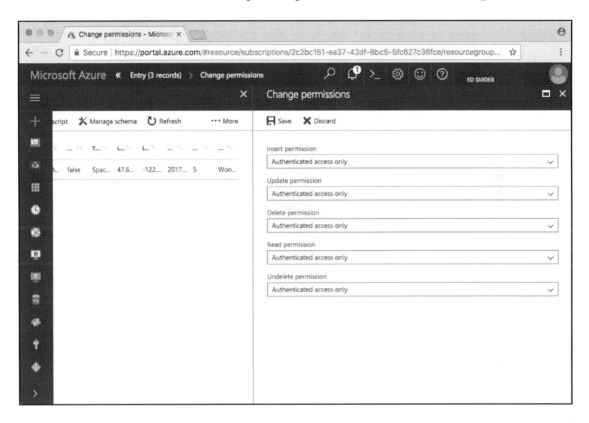

Now, any attempt to call the API endpoints, as we did in the previous chapter, will result in a 401 response. For example, using either a REST console or the command line, issue a GET request to the API endpoint for the Entry table using the following URL and header:

```
https://<your-service-name>.azurewebsites.net/tables/entry
--header "zumo-api-version:2.0.0"
```

You should now get back the following response message since we are not providing any valid authentication token in the request:

```
You must be logged in to use this application
```

In the next section, we will set up Facebook as an identity provider for our Azure App Service so that we can obtain a user-specific access token that can be used in the request headers, allowing us to get back a successful response.

Setting up an identity provider

There are a couple of approaches to handle identity and authentication in Azure. You can set up the Azure Mobile App Service to use Facebook, Twitter, Microsoft Account, Google, or even Azure Active Directory as a trusted identity provider. You can also create your own custom identity provider if you want to use account data stored in your database instead of one of the social providers. You can use one of these options or a combination of several of them—they will all provide an access token that can be used by your mobile app to communicate with your API on behalf of your users. In this section, we will use only one provider, Facebook.

In order to use a social network as an identity provider, you will need to have an app/client ID and app secret. These keys can be obtained directly from the identity provider by setting up an app for OAuth, typically in their developer portal. Once you have obtained the app/client ID and secret, you can configure the authentication settings for the backend service, as shown in the following steps:

1. Select your TripLog App Service in the Azure portal.
2. Click on **Authentication / Authorization** in the **MOBILE** section on the left side of the pane, as shown in the following screenshot:

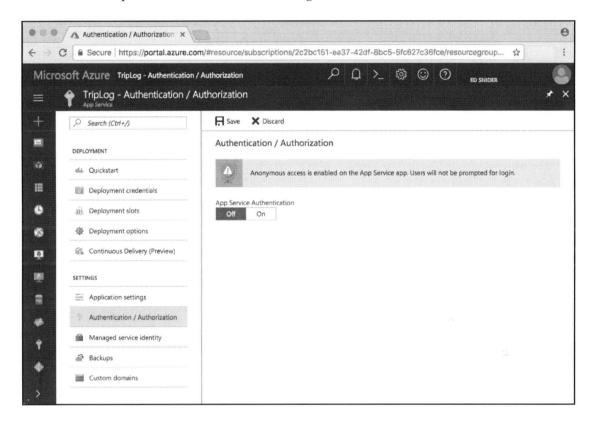

3. Switch the **App Service Authentication** toggle to **On**, as shown in the following screenshot:

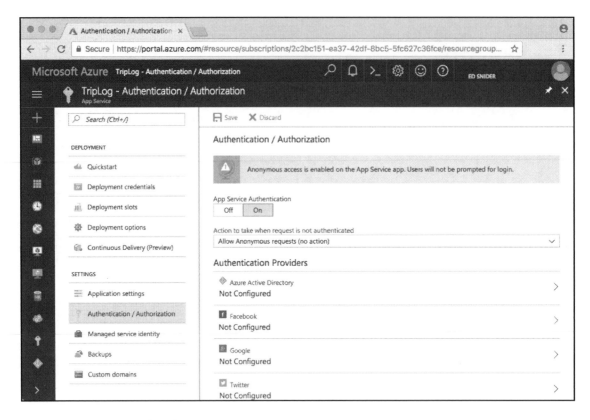

4. Select **Facebook**.

5. Provide your Facebook **App ID** and **App Secret** and click on the **OK** button at the bottom of the Facebook pane, as shown in the following screenshot:

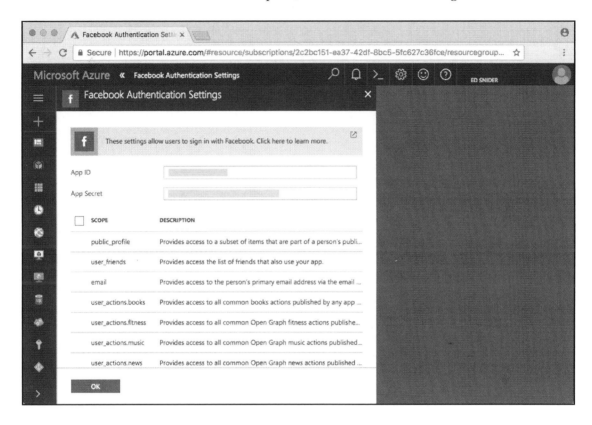

6. Click on the **Save** button at the top of the **Authentication / Authorization** pane.

7. Next, you will need to add the OAuth redirect **Uniform Resource Identifier (URI)** for your service within the app setting of the identity provider. The redirect URI will depend on the identity provider using the following format: `https://<your-service-name>.azurewebsites.net/.auth/login/<identity-provider>/callback`. Replace `<your-service-name>` with the name of your Azure Mobile App, and replace `<identity-provider>` with `facebook`, `twitter`, `microsoftaccount`, `google`, or `aad`, depending on which identity provider you are using.

> Setting up an app for OAuth is different for each provider, and the Azure App Service documentation has outlined the steps in detail for each, as follows:
>
> Facebook: `https://docs.microsoft.com/en-us/azure/app-service/app-service-mobile-how-to-configure-facebook-authentication/`
>
> Twitter: `https://docs.microsoft.com/en-us/azure/app-service/app-service-mobile-how-to-configure-twitter-authentication/`
>
> Microsoft account: `https://docs.microsoft.com/en-us/azure/app-service/app-service-mobile-how-to-configure-microsoft-authentication/`
>
> Google: `https://docs.microsoft.com/en-us/azure/app-service/app-service-mobile-how-to-configure-google-authentication/`
>
> Azure Active Directory: `https://docs.microsoft.com/en-us/azure/app-service/app-service-mobile-how-to-configure-active-directory-authentication/`

Once you have set everything up on the identity provider side and provided the keys in the Azure portal, you can test it out in your internet browser by navigating to `https://<your-service-name>.azurewebsites.net/.auth/login/facebook`.

If everything is set up correctly, you should see the login prompt for the identity provider. After providing your credentials, you should be prompted to give your app permission to use your account, as shown in the following screenshot:

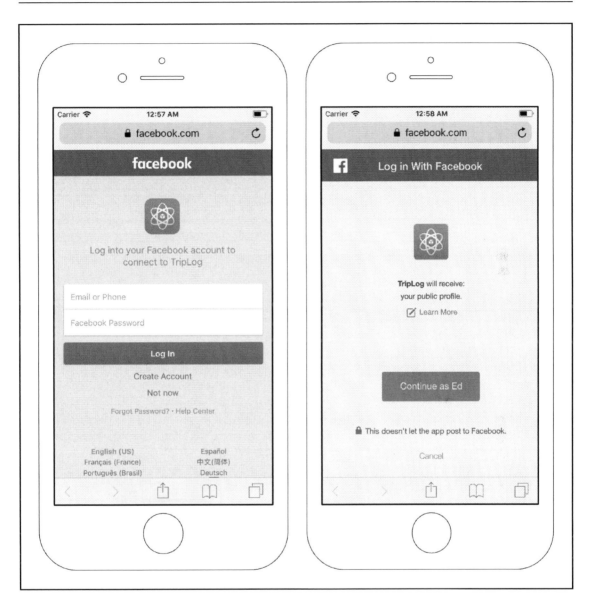

If you observe the URL in the browser address bar after clicking the Continue button, you should see the redirected URL appended with a token value in the form of a URL-encoded JSON object. We can then take the value of the `authenticationToken` key in that JSON object and use it in a request to our API to confirm that we get back a successful response.

In either a REST console or the command line, issue the same GET request that we did in the previous section, but this time, add a new header named x-zumo-auth and use the value from authenticationToken in the JSON object returned in the redirect URI as the x-zumo-auth header value:

```
https://<your-service-name>.azurewebsites.net/tables/entry
--header "zumo-api-version:2.0.0"
--header "x-zumo-auth:<your-authentication-token>"
```

If everything has been set up correctly, you should get back a response containing all of the Entry objects in the Azure backend service.

In the next section, we will update the TripLog app with a Facebook authentication page to get an access token that can be stored and used by the app to communicate with the API.

Creating an authentication service

Now that we have enabled our backend service with Facebook authentication, the app as it is from the previous chapter will fail to load content. In this section, we will update the app to authenticate users with Facebook via OAuth and obtain an access token from Azure that can be used in subsequent API calls by the TripLogApiDataService.

As in the previous chapter, instead of using the Azure Mobile Apps client SDK, we will directly call the REST endpoints behind the SDK to better understand the approach to authenticate to an API in a more generic way. In order to do this, we will first make an OAuth call to Facebook, obtaining a Facebook token. We will then pass that token to an Azure Mobile App Service endpoint, where it is validated using the Facebook app ID and secret that were added to the service's configuration in Azure to finally receive the access token needed to make calls to the API table endpoints.

Performing OAuth in a mobile app requires a certain set of platform-specific capabilities. So, we will need to follow the same pattern that we did in earlier chapters, as follows:

1. First, create a new interface named IAuthService in the Services folder in the core library:

```
public interface IAuthService
{
}
```

2. Update the `IAuthService` interface with a single method that takes in all the key components of a standard OAuth call as its parameters:

```
public interface IAuthService
{
    Task SignInAsync(string clientId,
                     Uri authUrl,
                     Uri callbackUrl,
                     Action<string> tokenCallback,
                     Action<string> errorCallback);
}
```

The two callback `Action` parameters provide a way to handle both success and failure OAuth responses.

Next, we will need to create an implementation of this interface. Just as we did with the geolocation service in Chapter 4, *Platform Specific Services and Dependency Injection*, we will leverage a Xamarin NuGet package to create the actual platform-specific implementation for `IAuthService`. The Xamarin.Auth library provides an easy-to-use cross-platform API to conduct OAuth in Xamarin mobile apps, as shown in the following steps:

1. Add the **Xamarin.Auth** NuGet package to each of the platform projects (that is, `TripLog.iOS`, `TripLog.Droid`, and so on).

2. Next, create a new class named `AuthService` in the `Services` folder in the `TripLog.iOS` project:

```
public class AuthService : IAuthService
{
}
```

3. Next, provide the implementation of the `SignInAsync` method:

```
public class AuthService : IAuthService
{
    public async Task SignInAsync(string clientId,
                                  Uri authUrl,
                                  Uri callbackUrl,
                                  Action<string> tokenCallback,
                                  Action<string> errorCallback)
    {
        var auth = new OAuth2Authenticator(clientId, string.Empty,
authUrl, callbackUrl);
        auth.AllowCancel = true;
        var controller = auth.GetUI();
```

```
            await UIApplication.SharedApplication
                              .KeyWindow
                              .RootViewController
                              .PresentViewControllerAsync(controller,
    true);

            auth.Completed += (s, e) =>
            {
                controller.DismissViewController(true, null);

                if (e.Account != null && e.IsAuthenticated)
                {
                    tokenCallback?.Invoke(
                        e.Account.Properties["access_token"]);
                }
                else
                {
                    errorCallback?.Invoke("Not authenticated");
                }
            };

            auth.Error += (s, e) =>
            {
                controller.DismissViewController(true, null);

                if (errorCallback != null)
                    errorCallback(e.Message);
            };
        }
    }
```

4. Finally, update the `TripLogPlatformModule` Ninject module in each platform-specific project to register its `IAuthService` implementation in the IoC:

```
public class TripLogPlatformModule : NinjectModule
{
    public override void Load()
    {
        Bind<ILocationService>().To<LocationService>()
                                .InSingletonScope();

        Bind<IAuthService>().To<AuthService>()
                            .InSingletonScope();
    }
}
```

The IAuthService interface provides a way to perform OAuth against Facebook, which gives us a Facebook authentication token, but we still need a way to pass that Facebook-specific token to our API to get back an Azure-authenticated access token that we can use in our API requests. Azure Mobile Apps provides an endpoint that takes an identity provider-specific token, and in return, provides back an Azure-specific access token. In order to use this endpoint, we just need to update our TripLog data service with a new method, as follows:

1. First, create a new model class named TripLogApiAuthToken. As we saw in the preceding section, the response from the /.auth/login/facebook endpoint is a JSON object containing a user object and an authenticationToken object; so, this TripLogApiAuthToken model will represent that structure so that we can deserialize the response and use the access token for future calls to the TripLog backend service:

```
public class TripLogApiUser
{
    public string UserId { get; set; }
}

public class TripLogApiAuthToken
{
    public TripLogApiUser User { get; set; }
    public string AuthenticationToken { get; set; }
}
```

2. Next, add a new method to the ITripLogDataService interface named GetAuthTokenAsync that returns an object of the TripLogApiAuthToken type we just created:

```
public interface ITripLogDataService
{
    Task<TripLogApiAuthToken> GetAuthTokenAsync(string idProvider,
        string idProviderToken);
    Task<IList<TripLogEntry>> GetEntriesAsync();
    Task<TripLogEntry> GetEntryAsync(string id);
    Task<TripLogEntry> AddEntryAsync(TripLogEntry entry);
    Task<TripLogEntry> UpdateEntryAsync(TripLogEntry entry);
    Task RemoveEntryAsync(TripLogEntry entry);
}
```

Notice the idProvider parameter, which allows this method to be used for Azure social identity providers beyond just Facebook.

3. Next, update the `TripLogApiDataService` to include the implementation of the `GetAuthTokenAsync` method that we just added to `ITripLogDataService`. The method needs to make a POST call to the `/.auth/login/facebook` endpoint with the access token received from the OAuth response in the request body. The service endpoint expects the token in the body to be associated with a key named `access_token`. Since our base HTTP service handles serializing the message body data for us, we can simply create a struct to house the token that will be passed to the endpoint:

```
public class TripLogApiDataService
    : BaseHttpService, ITripLogDataService
{
    readonly Uri _baseUri;
    IDictionary<string, string> _headers;

    // ...

    struct IdProviderToken
    {
        [JsonProperty("access_token")]
        public string AccessToken { get; set; }
    }

    public async Task<TripLogApiAuthToken> GetAuthTokenAsync(string
idProvider, string idProviderToken)
    {
        var token = new IdProviderToken
        {
            AccessToken = idProviderToken
        };

        var url = new Uri(_baseUri, string.Format(".auth/login/{0}",
idProvider));
        var response = await
SendRequestAsync<TripLogApiAuthToken>(url, HttpMethod.Post, _headers,
token);

        // Update this service with the new auth token
        if (response != null)
        {
            var authToken = response.AuthenticationToken;
            _headers["x-zumo-auth"] = authToken;
        }

        return response;
    }
```

```
    // ...
}
```

4. Finally, we will need to update the `TripLogApiDataService` constructor with a string parameter named `authToken`. In the `GetAuthTokenAsync` method, we will then need to update the `_headers` property within the service with token we received from the backend. However, we also need to be able to set the `_headers` property from the constructor so that we can initialize the service with a token if one already exists (for instance, if a token was persisted in the app's settings after signing in), as shown in the following code:

```
public TripLogApiDataService(Uri baseUri, string authToken)
{
    _baseUri = baseUri;
    _headers = new Dictionary<string, string> ();
    _headers.Add("zumo-api-version", "2.0.0");
    _headers.Add("x-zumo-auth", authToken);
}
```

Adding a sign in page

In order to add sign in capabilities to our app, we will need to create a new Page and a new ViewModel. The ViewModel will be pretty straightforward, containing just a single command that handles signing in to Facebook via the `IAuthService` interface, passing the received Facebook token to the Azure backend service through the `ITripLogDataService`, and then storing the Azure access token in local settings.

There are a couple of ways to tap into the local storage platform-specific APIs to store settings. One way is to roll your own, similar to how we did the geolocation service: creating a core interface that is implemented uniquely per platform. Another alternative is to leverage a plugin or other third-party library that has already been created and published. In this section, we will use a plugin called **Settings Plugin for Xamarin and Windows**, available on NuGet as **Xam.Plugins.Settings** by James Montemagno:

1. Add the **Xam.Plugins.Settings** NuGet package to the core library and each of the platform-specific projects, and update the `Settings` static helper class in the core library according to the package's README file to include a string setting property named `TripLogApiAuthToken`, as follows:

```
public static class Settings
{
    private static ISettings AppSettings
```

```
    {
        get => CrossSettings.Current;
    }

    private const string ApiAuthTokenKey = "apitoken_key";
    private static readonly string AuthTokenDefault = string.Empty;

    public static string TripLogApiAuthToken
    {
        get => AppSettings.GetValueOrDefault(ApiAuthTokenKey,
AuthTokenDefault);
        set => AppSettings.AddOrUpdateValue(ApiAuthTokenKey, value);
    }
}
```

2. Create a new class that inherits from `BaseViewModel` named `SignInViewModel`
   in the `ViewModels` folder in the core library:

```
public class SignInViewModel : BaseViewModel
{
}
```

3. Update the `SignInViewModel` with a constructor that takes in `INavService`,
   `IAuthService`, and `ITripLogDataService` parameters:

```
public class SignInViewModel : BaseViewModel
{
    readonly IAuthService _authService;
    readonly ITripLogDataService _tripLogService;

    public SignInViewModel(INavService navService,
                           IAuthService authService,
                           ITripLogDataService tripLogService)
        :base(navService)
    {
        _authService = authService;
        _tripLogService = tripLogService;
    }
}
```

4. Next, add a new `ICommand` property named `SignInCommand` to the
   `SignInViewModel` along with its execute `Action`:

```
public class SignInViewModel : BaseViewModel
{
    // ...
```

```
ICommand _signInCommand;
public ICommand SignInCommand
{
    get
    {
        return _signInCommand
            ?? (_signInCommand = new Command(
                async () => await ExecuteSignInCommand()));
    }
}

async Task ExecuteSignInCommand()
{
    // TODO: Update with your Facebook Client Id
    await _authService.SignInAsync("YOUR_FACEBOOK_CLIENTID",
        new Uri("https://m.facebook.com/dialog/oauth"),
        new
Uri("https://<your-service-name>.azurewebsites.net/.auth/login/facebook/cal
lback"),
            tokenCallback: async t =>
            {
                // Use Facebook token to get Azure auth token
                var response = await _tripLogService
                    .GetAuthTokenAsync("facebook", t);

                // Save auth token in local settings
                Helpers.Settings.TripLogApiAuthToken =
                    response.AuthenticationToken;

                // Navigate to Main
                await NavService.NavigateTo<MainViewModel>();
                await NavService.RemoveLastView ();
            },
            errorCallback: e =>
            {
                // TODO: Handle invalid authentication here
            });
    }
}
```

5. Override the `BaseViewModel Init()` method to clear the navigation back stack anytime the `SignInViewModel` is loaded:

```
public override async Task Init()
{
    await NavService.ClearBackStack();
}
```

6. Update the `TripLogCoreModule` Ninject module to add `SignInViewModel` to the IoC container:

```
public class TripLogCoreModule : NinjectModule
{
    public override void Load()
    {
        // ViewModels
        Bind<SignInViewModel>().ToSelf();
        Bind<MainViewModel>().ToSelf();
        Bind<DetailViewModel>().ToSelf();
        Bind<NewEntryViewModel>().ToSelf();

        // ...

    }
}
```

7. Update the `TripLogCoreModule` to account for the updated `TripLogApiDataService` constructor and pass in the auth token stored in local settings:

```
public class TripLogCoreModule : Ninject.Modules.NinjectModule
{
    public override void Load()
    {

        // ...

        var tripLogService = new TripLogApiDataService(new
            Uri("https://<your-service-name>.azurewebsites.net"),
            Helpers.Settings.TripLogApiAuthToken);

        // ...
    }
}
```

Next, we will need to create the actual sign in page, which will use the `SignInViewModel` as its data context:

1. Create a new XAML page in the `Views` folder in the core library named `SignInPage`.

2. Update the XAML of the `SignInPage` to add a button that is bound to `SignInCommand` of `SignInViewModel`:

```
<ContentPage.Content>
    <Button Text="Sign in with Facebook"
        BackgroundColor="#455c9f"
        TextColor="White"
        Command="{Binding SignInCommand}"
        Margin="20"
        VerticalOptions="Center" />
</ContentPage.Content>
```

3. Next, register the `SignInPage` and `SignInViewModel` mappings in the navigation service in the `TripLogNavModule` Ninject module:

```
public class TripLogNavModule : NinjectModule
{

    // ...

    public override void Load()
    {
        var navService = new XamarinFormsNavService();
        navService.XamarinFormsNav = _xfNav;

        // Register view mappings
        navService.RegisterViewMapping(
            typeof(SignInViewModel), typeof(SignInPage));

        navService.RegisterViewMapping(
            typeof(MainViewModel), typeof(MainPage));

        navService.RegisterViewMapping(
            typeof(DetailViewModel), typeof(DetailPage));

        navService.RegisterViewMapping(
            typeof(NewEntryViewModel), typeof(NewEntryPage));

        Bind<INavService>()
            .ToMethod(x => navService)
            .InSingletonScope();
    }
}
```

Finally, we will need to make two minor adjustments to the app so that users will go directly to the `SignInPage` if an auth token does not exist in local settings:

1. First, add a public `bool` property to the `App` class in `App.xaml.cs` that indicates whether an auth token is present by checking the `Settings` helper class:

```
public partial class App : Application
{

    // ...

    public bool IsSignedIn
    {
        get
        {
            return
                !string.IsNullOrWhiteSpace
                    (Helpers.Settings.TripLogApiAuthToken);
        }
    }

    // ...

}
```

2. Next, update the `Init` method of the `MainViewModel` to forward the user to the `SignInViewModel` if the `IsSignedIn` property is false:

```
public override async Task Init()
{
    if (!((App)Application.Current).IsSignedIn)
    {
        await NavService.NavigateTo<SignInViewModel>();
    }
    else
    {
        LoadEntries();
    }
}
```

Now, when the app is launched for the first time and an auth token is not present in the local settings, you will see the `SignInPage`. Clicking on the sign in button will launch the Xamarin.Auth dialog, prompting for Facebook credentials and permission to grant access to the TripLog app, as shown in the following screenshots:

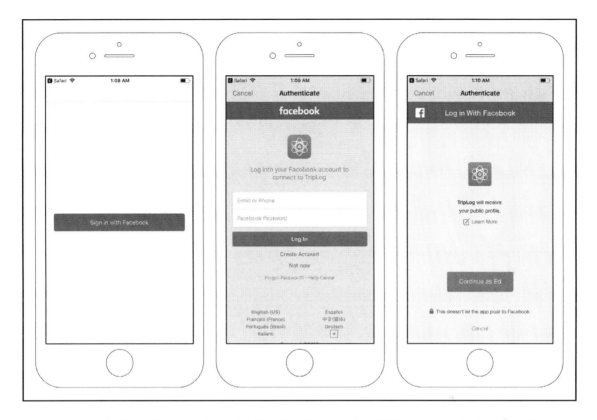

Upon successfully authenticating with Facebook, you should be automatically brought to the `MainPage` and the list of the Entry objects will be loaded from the API.

Summary

In this chapter, we updated the Azure backend service we created in the previous chapter with Facebook-provided identity. We also updated the API data service in the TripLog app to authenticate its HTTP API requests with a user-specific auth token provided by the Azure Mobile App Service, given a valid Facebook access token. Finally, we added a sign in page and updated the app to automatically route the user to the sign in page if an auth token isn't found in local settings.

In the next chapter, we will create unit tests for our TripLog app.

8
Testing

Throughout this book, we have implemented patterns and best practices with the intention of separating the layers of our TripLog app, making it easier to maintain and test. In this chapter, we will write unit tests for the business logic in our ViewModels.

Unit testing

To test the business logic in our TripLog app we will start out by creating a new unit test project in our solution that will be responsible for testing our ViewModels. There are many options and libraries to create unit tests in .NET with Visual Studio. In this chapter we will use the NUnit Library Project template in Visual Studio for Mac.

In order to create a unit test project, perform the following steps:

1. Create a new solution folder in the TripLog solution named Tests. Although this is not required, it helps keep any testing-related projects organized within the overall solution. To add a new solution folder in Visual Studio, simply right-click on the solution name, go to **Add** and click on **Add Solution Folder**, as shown in the following screenshot:

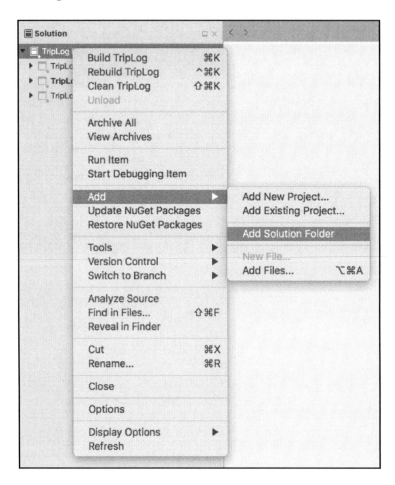

Adding a new solution folder in Visual Studio for Windows is the same process: right-click on the solution name, go to **Add** and click on **New Solution Folder**.

2. Next, create a new NUnit Library Project within the new `Tests` solution folder:

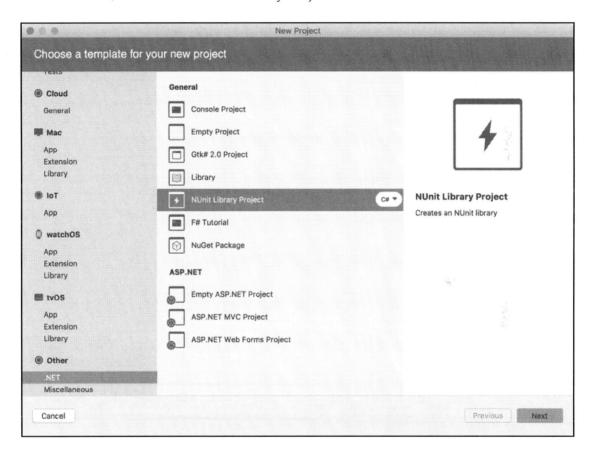

3. Name the NUnit Library Project `TripLog.Tests`, as shown in the following screenshot:

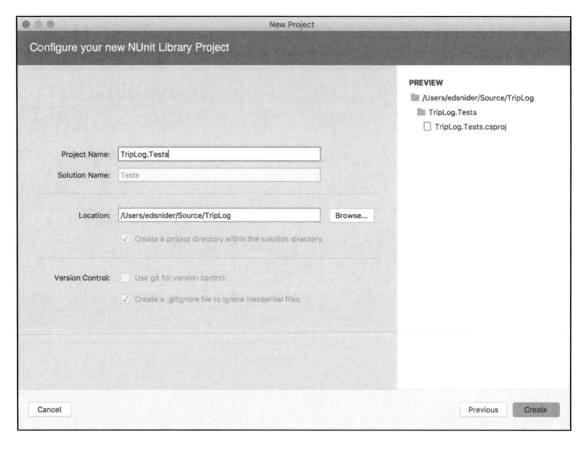

By default, the new NUnit project will contain a `Test.cs` file. You can safely delete this file, as we will create new ones that are specific to each of our ViewModels in the next section.

Testing ViewModels

When unit testing ViewModels, it is best to break the tests into individual test classes that represent each ViewModel, resulting in a one-to-one relationship between ViewModel classes and the unit test classes that test their logic.

In order to test our ViewModels, we will need to add a reference to them within the unit tests project, as shown in the following screenshot:

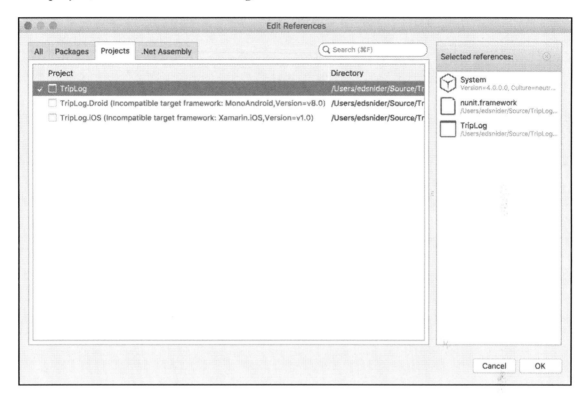

We will start by creating a set of unit tests for `DetailViewModel`:

1. First, create a new folder in the `TripLog.Tests` project named `ViewModels`. This helps keep the file structure of the tests the same as the library being tested.
2. Next, create a new empty class named `DetailViewModelTests` within the new `ViewModels` folder in the `TripLog.Tests` project.
3. Next, update the `DetailViewModelTests` class with a `TestFixture` attribute:

```
[TestFixture]
public class DetailViewModelTests
{
}
```

4. Then, create a test setup method in the `DetailViewModelTests` class by adding a new method named `Setup` with the `[SetUp]` NUnit attribute, as follows:

```
[TestFixture]
public class DetailViewModelTests
{
    [SetUp]
    public void Setup()
    {
    }
}
```

This `Setup` method will be responsible for creating new instances of our ViewModel for each of the tests within the class by ensuring that each test is run with a clean, known state of the ViewModel under test.

In order to create a new instance of a ViewModel, we will need to provide it with the instances of the services required by its constructor. During runtime, these are automatically provided via constructor injection, but in the case of the unit tests, we will need to provide them manually. We have a couple of options for passing in these services. We can create new mock versions of our services and pass them into the ViewModel's constructor. This requires providing a mock implementation for each method in the service's interface, which can be time-consuming and causes additional code maintenance. We can also use a mocking library to create mocks of the services and pass these mocks into the ViewModel's constructor. The mocking library provides a much cleaner approach that is also less fragile. Additionally, most mocking libraries will provide a way to specify how methods or properties should return data in a much cleaner way without actually having to implement them ourselves. I like to use **Moq** (available on NuGet)—a very popular mocking library for .NET applications—to handle mocking for my unit tests.

In order to initialize the ViewModel with mocked services, perform the following steps:

1. Add a reference to the **Moq** NuGet package to the TripLog.Tests project.
2. Next, within the `Setup` method, create a new instance of `DetailViewModel` and use the Moq library to create a mock instance of `INavService` to pass in when instantiating `DetailViewModel`:

```
[TestFixture]
public class DetailViewModelTests
{
    DetailViewModel _vm;

    [SetUp]
    public void Setup()
```

```
        {
            var navMock = new Mock<INavService>().Object;
            _vm = new DetailViewModel(navMock);
        }
    }
```

Now that we have a setup function defined, we can create an actual test method. This ViewModel does not do much beyond initialization. Therefore, we will just test the Init method to ensure that the ViewModel is properly initialized when its Init method is called. The success criteria for this particular test will be that once Init is called, the Entry property of the ViewModel will be set to the value provided in the Init method's parameter.

In order to create a test for the ViewModel's Init method, perform the following steps:

1. Create a new method in DetailViewModelTests named Init_ParameterProvided_EntryIsSet and decorate it with an NUnit Test attribute. Each test method that we create will follow the **Arrange-Act-Assert** pattern:

```
[TestFixture]
public class DetailViewModelTests
{
    // ...

    [Test]
    public async Task Init_ParameterProvided_EntryIsSet()
    {
        // Arrange

        // Act

        // Assert
    }
}
```

2. Next, update the arrange portion of the test method by creating a new mocked instance of a TripLogEntry object to pass to the Init method in order to test its functionality. Also, set the ViewModel's Entry property to null so that we can easily confirm that the property has a proper value after calling Init later in the assert portion of the test, as follows:

```
[Test]
public async Task Init_ParameterProvided_EntryIsSet()
{
```

```
    // Arrange
    var mockEntry = new Mock<TripLogEntry>().Object;
    _vm.Entry = null;

    // Act

    // Assert
}
```

3. Next, pass the mocked `TripLogEntry` object into the ViewModel's `Init` method in the act portion of the test method:

```
[Test]
public async Task Init_ParameterProvided_EntryIsSet()
{
    // Arrange
    var mockEntry = new Mock<TripLogEntry>().Object;
    _vm.Entry = null;

    // Act
    await _vm.Init(mockEntry);

    // Assert
}
```

4. Finally, verify that the ViewModel's `Entry` property is no longer `null` using the NUnit `Assert.IsNotNull` method:

```
[Test]
public async Task Init_ParameterProvided_EntryIsSet()
{
    // Arrange
    var mockEntry = new Mock<TripLogEntry>().Object;
    _vm.Entry = null;

    // Act
    await _vm.Init(mockEntry);

    // Assert
    Assert.IsNotNull(_vm.Entry, "Entry is null after being
initialized with a valid TripLogEntry object");
}
```

TIP There are several other `Assert` methods, such as `AreEqual`, `IsTrue`, and `IsFalse`, that can be used for various types of assertions.

Notice the second parameter in the `Assert.IsNotNull` method usage in step 4, which is an optional parameter. This allows you to provide a message to be displayed if the test fails to help troubleshoot the code under the test.

We should also include a test to ensure that the ViewModel throws an exception if the empty `Init` method is called, because the `DetailViewModel` requires the use of the `Init` method in the base class that takes a parameter. We can do this using the `Assert.Throws` NUnit method and providing a delegate that calls the `Init` method:

```
[Test]
public void Init_ParameterNotProvided_ThrowsEntryNotProvidedException()
{
    // Assert
    Assert.Throws(typeof(EntryNotProvidedException), async () =>
        {
            await _vm.Init();
        });
}
```

Initially, this test will fail because until this point, we have not included the code to throw an `EntryNotProvidedException` in `DetailViewModel`. In fact, the tests currently will not even build because we have not defined the `EntryNotProvidedException` type.

In order to get the tests to build, create a new class in the core library that inherits from `Exception` and name it `EntryNotProvidedException`:

```
public class EntryNotProvidedException : Exception
{
    public EntryNotProvidedException()
        : base("An Entry object was not provided. If using DetailViewModel,
    be sure to use the Init overload that takes an Entry parameter.")
    {
    }
}
```

For ViewModels that have dependencies on a specific functionality of a service, you will need to provide some additional setup when you mock the objects for its constructor. For example, the NewEntryViewModel depends on the GetGeoCoordinatesAsync method of ILocationService in order to get the user's current location in the Init method. By simply providing a new Mock object for ILocationService to ViewModel, this method will return null, and an exception will be thrown when setting the Latitude and Longitude properties.

In order to overcome this, we will just need to use the Setup method when creating Mock to define how the calls to the GetGeoCoordinatesAsync method should be returned to the callers of the mock ILocationService instance:

1. Create a new class in the TripLog.Tests project named NewEntryViewModelTests. Add the TextFixture attribute to the class, just as we did with the DetailViewModelTests class:

```
[TestFixture]
public class NewEntryViewModelTests
{
}
```

2. Next, create a method named Setup with the SetUp attribute, where we will define the NewEntryViewModel instance that will be used by tests in the class. NewEntryViewModel requires three parameters. We will use Moq again to provide mock implementations for them, but we will need to customize the implementation for ILocationService to specify exactly what the GetGeoCoordinatesAsync method should return:

```
[TestFixture]
public class NewEntryViewModelTests
{
    NewEntryViewModel _vm;

    [SetUp]
    public void Setup()
    {
        var navMock = new Mock<INavService>();
        var dataMock = new Mock<ITripLogDataService>();
        var locMock = new Mock<ILocationService>();
        locMock.Setup(x => x.GetGeoCoordinatesAsync())
            .ReturnsAsync(new GeoCoords
            {
                Latitude = 123,
                Longitude = 321
```

```
                         });

            _vm = new NewEntryViewModel(navMock.Object,
                                        locMock.Object,
                                        dataMock.Object);
        }
    }
```

Now that we know our mock ILocationService implementation will return 123 for Latitude and 321 for Longitude, we can properly test the ViewModel's Init method and ensure that the Latitude and Longitude properties are properly set using its provided ILocationService (this would be an actual platform-specific implementation when running the mobile app).

Following the Arrange-Act-Assert pattern, set the values of the Latitude and Longitude properties to 0 before calling the Init method. In the assert portion of the test, confirm that after calling Init, the Latitude and Longitude properties of ViewModel are the values that we expect to come from the provided mock ILocationService instance—in our case, 123 and 321:

```
[TestFixture]
public class NewEntryViewModelTests
{
    // ...

    [Test]
    public async Task Init_EntryIsSetWithGeoCoordinates()
    {
        // Arrange
        _vm.Latitude = 0.0;
        _vm.Longitude = 0.0;

        // Act
        await _vm.Init();

        // Assert
        Assert.AreEqual(123, _vm.Latitude);
        Assert.AreEqual(321, _vm.Longitude);
    }
}
```

It is important to recognize that we are not testing the actual result or functionality of the `ILocationService` method—we are testing the behavior of the `Init` method which depends on the `ILocationService` method. The best way to do this is with mock objects—especially for platform-specific services or services that provide dynamic or inconsistent data.

As you can see in the preceding code, the use of dependency injection in the app architecture makes it extremely easy to test our ViewModels with maximum flexibility and minimum code.

Running unit tests in Visual Studio

Once you have some unit tests created, you can start running them directly from Visual Studio. Typically, this should be done as tests are created throughout your development lifecycle as well as before you commit your code to source control, especially if there is a continuous integration process that will automatically build your code and run the tests.

After the tests have completed running, the results will appear in the **Test Results** pane:

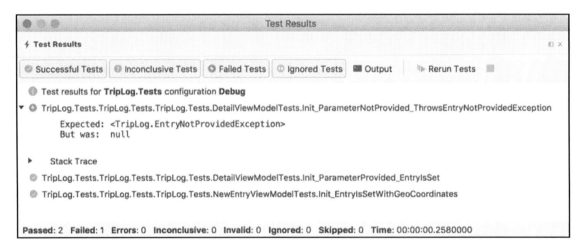

Notice (in the preceding screenshot) that one of our unit tests is failing. In order to get this test to pass, we will need to go back and update `DetailViewModel` by overriding the empty `Init` method of `BaseViewModel` and have it throw a new `EntryNotProvidedException` instance, as follows; this type of iterative testing development process is a common best practice that helps you develop better code with more testing coverage:

```
public class DetailViewModel : BaseViewModel<TripLogEntry>
{
    // ...

    public override async Task Init()
    {
        throw new EntryNotProvidedException();
    }

    public override async Task Init(TripLogEntry logEntry)
    {
        Entry = logEntry;
    }
}
```

Now, when you rerun the unit tests, they should all pass:

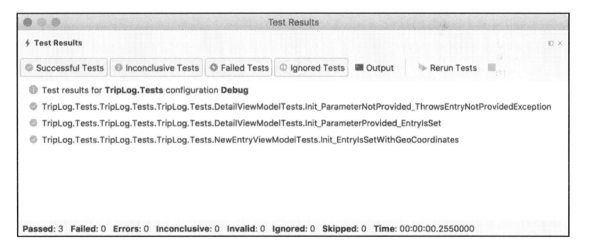

Summary

In this chapter, we looked into how to take advantage of the loosely coupled architecture that we have developed in the earlier chapters of this book to write unit tests. We used a mocking framework to mock out the services that our ViewModels are dependent on to be able to effectively test the logic within them in a predictable manner. In the next chapter we will add the ability to monitor app usage and crashes in our TripLog mobile app.

9
App Monitoring

In the mobile development world, it is very important to iterate fast—users want new features and expect quality, and if you cannot deliver on those expectations, you will certainly feel it in your ratings and reviews. One of the best ways to ensure that you are shipping quality apps and features is to employ **DevOps**. DevOps is where the technical and operational sides of app development meet. Proper DevOps integrates business operations with tools, resulting in a more automated and continuous release process. DevOps tools typically combine **continuous integration and delivery (CI/CD)**—automation of the building, testing, and distributing of your app and monitoring it. CI/CD and monitoring together create a seamless loop where CI/CD provides an output of testable features, and monitoring provides an input of feedback and analytics on those features. This continuous loop, when implemented properly, enables development teams to rapidly release new features that maintain the quality their users expect.

In this last chapter of the book, we will focus on analytics and crash reporting tools and how they can help you continuously monitor and improve your app. Specifically, we will take a look at **Visual Studio App Center** and how to integrate its SDK libraries into the TripLog Xamarin.Forms mobile app that we have created in this book.

In this chapter, we will cover the following topics:

- Mobile app analytics and crash reporting
- Adding the Visual Studio App Center SDK to the TripLog app

Mobile app analytics and crash reporting

Application analytics and crash reporting tools have been around for a long time. The idea of application analytics is to collect data about your users, their behavior within your application, the features they use (or don't use), and how often they use the application or specific features of the application. The idea of crash reporting is to collect crash or error data from within the application. In both cases, the information collected is typically aggregated into a single dashboard-like interface so that you and other members on the application team can analyze it.

Application analytics are also extremely important to a product's life cycle and its stakeholders, as it provides real insight into the application and can help drive key business decisions around the product. For example, a feature that was thought to be very important to users might show up in analytics data as something that users are not actually using as much as anticipated. From there, the decision needs to be made whether this is because the feature is undiscoverable or simply not as important to the users as anticipated. On the other hand, analytics might indicate that a specific feature or area within your application is being used or accessed far more than expected. This would tell the product owners and developers that focusing on that feature or area should be a priority.

The power of a crash reporting tool is that it automatically captures the exception and stack trace information. Without this type of capability, you, as a developer, are left to rely on your end user to report the bug or error. In some cases, they may not even report the error and will simply close your app, and you will have no idea the bug even exists. Assuming that your users do report back to you about a bug or error they witnessed in the application, you are still relying on them to provide you with accurate information and are left trying to reproduce the error. Not only is this a potentially inaccurate process, but it is also time-consuming and cumbersome. It puts a burden on your users, as well as you and your development team. Having a crash reporting tool in place allows you to handle bugs and errors in real time, which is much faster than relying on users. If a user does experience a bug and reports it to you, having the crash reporting tool integrated within your app allows you to easily find the data related to the error they ran into. Furthermore, if you have both app analytics and crash reporting in your application, you can often leverage the analytics to identify the specific path the user took within the application before running into the issue.

There are several tools on the market, some that only do analytics, others that only do crash reporting, and, of course, some that do both. Most of the tools support .NET, and several specifically support Xamarin, making it easy to integrate them into mobile applications built with Xamarin. Microsoft's Visual Studio App Center is a service that offers analytics, error, and crash reporting tools on top of a suite of automated build, distribution and testing tools.

Visual Studio App Center

Visual Studio App Center is a service provided by Microsoft that offers a comprehensive mobile DevOps toolchain. One of the biggest barriers to entry when it comes to setting up the DevOps tooling is the amount of configuration, integration, and maintenance that is involved. In my experience, setting up DevOps tools means integrating several services, writing tons of scripts, and typically dedicating a developer to maintaining the *build server*. App Center offers a streamlined solution that minimizes configuration and pretty much eliminates integration and maintenance since it is a centralized and hosted service.

All of the components of App Center can be accessed via the App Center website or API. The monitoring components also require the App Center SDK to be included in your mobile app package. For Xamarin apps, the SDK is available via NuGet.

 This chapter is primarily focused on the app monitoring tools within Visual Studio App Center. To learn more about all of the tools and features of Visual Studio App Center, visit `http://appcenter.ms`.

Setting up Visual Studio App Center

If you don't already have an App Center account, you'll need to create one. Once you have signed in to App Center, create a new *app* for each platform you will be delivering your mobile app on. Each app you create in the App Center will be associated with a unique identifier known as an *app secret*. These app secrets are required when using the App Center SDK within your mobile app.

Creating an analytics service

In order to use the App Center SDK in our TripLog app, we will want to abstract it into a service, like we did for geolocation. As we saw multiple times in previous chapters, there are numerous benefits to this approach, namely, it loosely couples our ViewModels from the actual code that uses the App Center SDK, making unit testing our ViewModels much simpler and cleaner.

In order to create an analytics service, perform the following steps:

1. First, create a new interface named `IAnalyticsService` in the `Services` folder of the core library:

   ```
   public interface IAnalyticsService
   {
   }
   ```

2. Next, update the `IAnalyticsService` interface with methods to track usage events and errors:

   ```
   public interface IAnalyticsService
   {
       void TrackEvent(string eventKey);
       void TrackEvent(string eventKey,
           IDictionary<string, string> data);
       void TrackError(Exception exception);
       void TrackError(Exception exception,
           IDictionary<string, string> data);
   }
   ```

Notice in the preceding code that the methods in this service are not necessarily specific to App Center—they represent a pretty generic functionality when it comes to event and error tracking. This leads to yet another benefit of the loosely coupled architecture that we have put in place: if, for some reason, you need to stop using App Center Analytics and use another app analytics toolset instead, you will need to simply write a new implementation of this interface, and your ViewModels will automatically be ready to use the new implementation since they use it through the `IAnalyticsService` interface. Unit tests for ViewModels that have a dependency on `IAnalyticsService` will also require no change if the concrete implementation changes, and they will provide validation that the ViewModels haven't started failing as a result of swapping out implementations.

For now, we will, of course, use App Center in our concrete implementation of the
`IAnalyticsService` interface. The App Center Analytics and Crashes API is pretty simple
and straightforward, and so the implementation for each of the methods in the interface is
no more than a couple of lines of code. Specifically, the `Analytics.TrackEvent` and
`Crashes.TrackError` methods allow us to send user events and exceptions to App
Center, which are then visible within the App Center website.

In order to create the App Center implementation of `IAnalyticsService`, perform the
following steps:

1. Add the **Microsoft.AppCenter.Analytics** and **Microsoft.AppCenter.Crashes**
   NuGet packages to the core project and each of the platform-specific projects.
2. Start the SDK using your provided app secrets for each platform in the
   `OnStart` method override in the `App` class (`App.xaml.cs`):

```
protected override void OnStart()
{
    AppCenter.Start("ios={Your iOS app secret here};"
        + "android={Your Android app secret here};"
        + "uwp={Your UWP app secret here}",
        typeof(Analytics), typeof(Crashes));
}
```

3. Create a new class named `AppCenterAnalyticsService` in the `Services`
   folder in the core library that implements `IAnalyticsService`:

```
public class AppCenterAnalyticsService : IAnalyticsService
{
}
```

4. Next, implement the members of `IAnalyticsService` within the
   `AppCenterAnalyticsService` class:

```
public class AppCenterAnalyticsService : IAnalyticsService
{
    public void TrackEvent(string eventKey)
    {
        Analytics.TrackEvent(eventKey);
    }

    public void TrackEvent(string eventKey,
        IDictionary<string, string> data)
    {
        Analytics.TrackEvent(eventKey, data);
    }
```

```
        public void TrackError(Exception exception)
        {
            Crashes.TrackError(exception);
        }

        public void TrackError(Exception exception,
            IDictionary<string, string> data)
        {
            Crashes.TrackError(exception, data);
        }
    }
```

5. Next, update the `TripLogCoreModule` Ninject Module in the core library to register the `AppCenterAnalyticsService` implementation into the IoC:

```
public class TripLogCoreModule : NinjectModule
{
    public override void Load()
    {
        // ViewModels

        // ...

        // Core Services

        // ...

        Bind<IAnalyticsService>()
            .To<AppCenterAnalyticsService>()
            .InSingletonScope();
    }
}
```

Next, we will need to be able to use this new analytics service within the logic of our app, specifically, the ViewModels. Since we will likely need to report analytics data from all of our ViewModels, it would be best to just include an instance of `IAnalyticsService` as a protected property of the `BaseViewModel`, similar to the `INavService` property, and include it in the constructor's parameter list:

```
public abstract class BaseViewModel : INotifyPropertyChanged
{
    protected INavService NavService { get; private set; }
    protected IAnalyticsService AnalyticsService { get; private set; }

    // ...

    protected BaseViewModel(INavService navService,
```

```
        IAnalyticsService analyticsService)
    {
        NavService = navService;
        AnalyticsService = analyticsService;
    }

    // ...
}
```

We will also need to update the constructor of the BaseViewModel<TParameter> class that subclasses BaseViewModel to take an IAnalyticsService parameter, which it simply passes to its base constructor:

```
public abstract class BaseViewModel<TParameter> : BaseViewModel
{
    protected BaseViewModel(INavService navService,
        IAnalyticsService analyticsService)
        : base(navService, analyticsService)
    {
    }

    // ...
}
```

Finally, we will need to update the constructors of each of the ViewModels that inherit from BaseViewModel to take an IAnalyticsService parameter, which is just passed to its BaseViewModel base class.

Tracking exceptions and events

Now that we have an IAnalyticsService property in all of our ViewModels, we can update all of our try/catch blocks to pass exceptions to App Center. For example, in MainViewModel, we have a try/finally block in the LoadEntries method that is currently not catching exceptions.

Update this try/finally block with a catch block and then pass any caught Exception off to the analytics service via the TrackError method:

```
void LoadEntries()
{
    if (IsBusy)
    {
        return;
    }
```

```
IsBusy = true;

try
{
    // ...
}
catch (Exception e)
{
    AnalyticsService.TrackError(e,
        new Dictionary<string, string>
        {
            {"Method", "MainViewModel.LoadEntries()"}
        });
}
finally
{
    IsBusy = false;
}
}
```

 The App Center Crashes SDK automatically reports all unhandled exceptions once it is enabled in the app.

We can also start tracking user events throughout the application. For example, if we wanted to know how often users viewed the entry detail page in our app, we could call the TrackEvent method of IAnalyticsService within the Init method of DetailViewModel to log that in App Center Analytics:

```
public class DetailViewModel : BaseViewModel<TripLogEntry>
{
    // ...

    public override async Task Init(TripLogEntry logEntry)
    {
        AnalyticsService.TrackEvent("Entry Detail Page",
            new Dictionary<string, string>
            {
                { "Title", logEntry.Title }
            });

        // ...

    }
}
```

Summary

In this chapter, we covered the importance of analytics and crash reporting capabilities in mobile apps. We built an analytics service that abstracts away a Visual Studio App Center SDK implementation details from our ViewModels.

Other Books You May Enjoy

If you enjoyed this book, you may be interested in these other books by Packt:

Mastering Cross-Platform Development with Xamarin
Can Bilgin

ISBN: 978-1-78528-568-4

- Configure your environment for cross-platform projects with Xamarin
- Gain memory management skills to avoid memory leaks and premature code cycles while decreasing the memory print of your applications
- Employ asynchronous and parallel patterns to execute non-interactive and non-blocking processes
- Create and use SQLite databases for offline scenarios
- Integrate network resources with cross-platform applications
- Design and implement eye-catching and reusable UI components without compromising nativity in mobile applications
- Manage the application lifecycle of cross-platform development projects
- Distribute Xamarin applications through public or private channels

Mastering Xamarin UI Development

Steven F. Daniel

ISBN: 978-1-78646-200-8

- Develop stunning native cross-platform apps using the Xamarin.Forms framework
- Work with the different UI layouts to create customized layouts using the C# programming language and tweak it for a given platform
- Customize the user interface using DataTemplates and CustomRenderers and the Platform Effects API to change the appearance of control elements
- Build hybrid apps using the Razor Template Engine and create Razor Models that communicate with a SQLite database
- Use location based features within your app to display the user's current location
- Work with the Xamarin.Forms Map control to display Pin placeholders based on the stored latitude and longitude coordinates
- Understand and use the MVVM pattern architecture to navigate between each of your ViewModels and implement Data Binding to display and update information
- Work with the Microsoft Azure Platform to incorporate API Data Access using Microsoft Azure App Services and the RESTful API
- Incorporate third-party features within your app using the Facebook SDK and the Open Graph API
- Perform unit testing and profile your Xamarin.Forms applications
- Deploy your apps to the Google Play Store and Apple App Store

Leave a review - let other readers know what you think

Please share your thoughts on this book with others by leaving a review on the site that you bought it from. If you purchased the book from Amazon, please leave us an honest review on this book's Amazon page. This is vital so that other potential readers can see and use your unbiased opinion to make purchasing decisions, we can understand what our customers think about our products, and our authors can see your feedback on the title that they have worked with Packt to create. It will only take a few minutes of your time, but is valuable to other potential customers, our authors, and Packt. Thank you!

Index

Printed in Great Britain
by Amazon